Active PE

Book 1

David Alldridge and Robert Fisher

STANLEY
THORNES

First published in the United Kingdom in 1994 by
Simon & Schuster Education

Reprinted in 1995 by
Stanley Thornes (Publishers) Ltd
Ellenborough House
Wellington Street
CHELTENHAM GL50 1YW
England

96 97 98 99 00 / 10 9 8 7 6 5 4 3 2

A catalogue record of this book is available from the British Library.

ISBN 0 7487 2397 8

Designed by Robert and Jean Wheeler Design Associates
Edited by Catherine Hardingham

Printed and bound in Great Britain by Ashford Colour Press

Contents

Introduction

Active PE aims to help teachers of primary-age children to implement the National Curriculum in planning, teaching and assessing physical education (PE). Book 1 covers Key Stage 1: the 5–7 age range (years reception, 1 and 2), and Book 2 covers Key Stage 2: the 7–11+ age range (years 3–6). Active PE offers developing units of work which will be of practical use to teachers in helping children to enjoy and succeed in all aspects of PE.

About this book

The units of Book 1 offer a comprehensive and complete scheme of work for the six areas of study in PE for Key Stage 1: gymnastics, dance, games, athletics, outdoor education and swimming. The section on assessment includes record sheets to help evaluate progress, which can be photocopied and used as an ongoing record of achievement for each child. You will also find a list of resources at the end of the book, giving information about relevant publications, and useful addresses.

Gymnastics, dance and games are seen as the core areas of PE in the primary school and should be experienced regularly by children (weekly if possible) throughout the year; Athletics can be linked to games, as many athletic skills fit easily into the games programme, especially running, jumping and throwing; Outdoor and adventurous activities ought, where possible, to be part of the daily experience of each child as outdoor play, and can be linked to many areas of learning; Swimming is an activity that schools may or may not choose to include at Key Stage 1, but it is a National Curriculum requirement that all children should have been taught to swim at least 25 metres by the end of Key Stage 2.

Active PE provides a broad-based PE programme that will help young children develop all aspects of the 'physical' child, and also help support social, conceptual and emotional development. The book shows how to present active, enjoyable and successful PE lessons, which will help children form positive attitudes to physical activity, and encourage lifelong health and fitness.

How to use this book

Each of the six units in this book contains the following sections: **What to teach** includes Statements of Attainment and Programmes of Study as outlined in the National Curriculum. These set out the statutory requirements in England and Wales for each teaching aspect of PE. This section provides a framework and reference point for long-term planning in PE, and for assessing the progress of individual children. Units of work are identified that aim to cover the Statements of Attainment and Programmes of Study for a year, or across a key stage. **Lesson planning** includes advice on how to prepare, organise and plan a lesson or series of lessons for each unit of work, within a suggested pattern of warm-up activity, skills development and conclusion. **Units of work** includes themes and suggested activities which will help to develop knowledge, skills and positive attitudes in PE. The activities are listed under key themes, with activities which progress in a suggested order, from simple to more complex tasks. You are invited to select those tasks you consider most suitable for the children in your class. **Assessment** and record-keeping advice is given in the section pp 111–116. **Resources** for each element of the PE curriculum are suggested in the section pp117–124. An index at the back of the book provides quick and easy reference to the key elements of PE-teaching contained in this book.

The **ACTIVE** in *Active PE* expresses the aims that we have in our teaching of PE, to offer children learning experiences that are:

A ctive   –promoting healthy, active lifestyles.
C o-operative   –teaching co-operation with others.
T houghtful   –encouraging planning, reflection and review.
I nventive   –fostering creativity in thought and movement.
V aried   –developing a variety of physical skills.
E njoyable   –gaining enjoyment and success from physical activity.

Why is PE important ?

There are many reasons why PE is important which can be summarised under three headings: the value of healthy exercise; the development of physical intelligence; and the growth of self-confidence

The value of healthy exercise

One of the most important reasons for PE is that it provides children with exercise. Reasons why exercise is important include:

- **Growth**: exercise is essential for physical growth, development and the healthy functioning of the various systems in the body.
- **Strength**: regular exercise leads to greater physical and muscular strength.
- **Suppleness**: varied experience of physical movements will increase suppleness, and the responsiveness of the body to physical challenge.
- **Stamina**: exercise improves the heart and cardiovascular system, which will help develop stamina and functional capacity.

Recent studies have revealed that many British children do not experience vigorous exercise in school, or in their out-of-school activities. This probably contributes to the low levels of fitness characteristic of many older schoolchildren. A priority for physical education is not only to ensure that children get exercise, but to help build up an awareness of health issues and the value of an active lifestyle. The body is like a machine that stays healthy with use; it needs to be cared for, and the exercise habit is one that we hope will stay with them throughout life.

The development of physical intelligence

Physical intelligence is made up of physical and mental skills (physical skills are more accurately called psycho-motor skills). These physical and mental skills are closely linked. Success in physical activity depends on intellectual skills such as concentration, judgement and close observation, as well as on creativity in thought and movement. Active PE means being active in mind and body; we need to encourage a thoughtful or 'mindful' approach to physical activity, including an awareness of self and of others. This has important practical consequences, since safety of self and others is best achieved through a 'think first' approach.

(For more on physical and other forms of intelligence see *Teaching Children to Think* by Robert Fisher, published by Simon & Schuster.)

The growth of self-confidence

The body is not simply a machine. It is a vehicle of a child's sense of self and self-worth. In making PE lessons enjoyable and satisfying, in providing opportunities for success and development of skills, we also help to build self-esteem and a sense of self-worth. Through PE we can give children physical confidence. We help to show them that they can do more than they think, and that they can do things well. In our lessons we value who they are and what they can achieve. Studies have shown the value of building self-esteem and high expectations in the development of positive attitudes to life and learning. A growing sense of confidence and physical control can help children to respond well to other forms of challenge, both in and out of school.

Fig 1: Aims of Physical Education

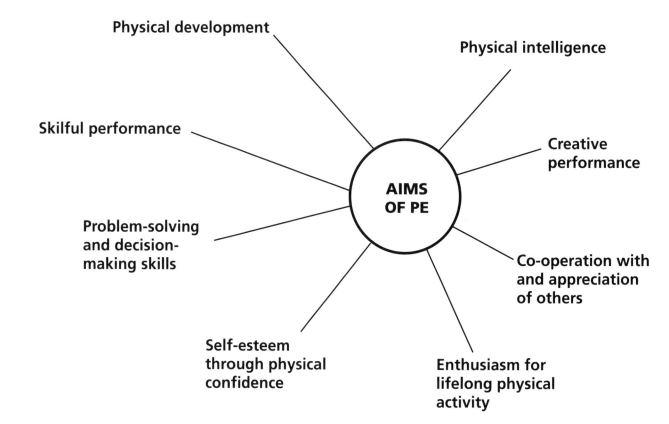

What should we teach ?

PE and the National Curriculum

'Physical education contributes to the overall education of young people by helping them to lead full and valuable lives through engaging in purposeful physical activity.' *(NCC PE in the National Curriculum, Non-Statutory Guidance 1992)*. The National Curriculum defines the basic entitlement of pupils to PE under three component headings:

- One attainment target (AT).
- End of key stage statements (EKSS).
- Programmes of study (PoS).

The attainment target

Physical Education in the National Curriculum (1992) states that the one attainment target for PE for pupils aged 5–16 shall be that 'pupils should be able to demonstrate the knowledge, skills and understanding involved in areas of activity encompassing athletic activities, dance, games, gymnastic activities, outdoor and adventurous activities and swimming'. This attainment target relates to the three basic processes of planning, performing and evaluating (plan-do-review) which should relate to all purposeful physical activity: **planning** involves thinking ahead, exploring options, setting goals, selecting, organising, creating and structuring physical practice; **performing** involves active participation, copying, practising, repeating, implementing a plan of action, refining, adapting, developing, improving and improvising; **evaluating** involves observing, describing (using word and action), analysing, comparing and contrasting, judging, reviewing, and recognising the effects of physical activities on their bodies.

These processes are expressed in the end of key stage statements which relate to the programme of study for Key Stage 1. Pupils should be able to:

- plan and perform safely a range of simple actions and linked movements in response to given tasks and stimuli;
- practise and improve their performance;
- describe what they and others are doing;
- recognise the effects of physical activities on their bodies.

(PE in the National Curriculum, 1992)

Programme of study (PoS)

These define both general requirements about what the pupils should have opportunities to learn and experience, as well as the specific areas of activity: gymnastics; games; athletics; dance; outdoor and adventurous activity; swimming (which can be taught at Key Stage 1).

The general statements in the PoS reflect the importance within PE of three elements which should permeate all activities:

Personal and social development

In order to help pupils become independent learners, they should be encouraged to solve for themselves the problems they encounter in the course of physical activities. In order to develop positive attitudes, pupils should be encouraged to observe the conventions of fair play, honest competition and good sporting behaviour; understand and cope with a variety of outcomes, including success and failure; and be aware of the effects and consequences of their actions on others and on the environment.

Safety

To help ensure safe practice, pupils should be taught to:

* be concerned with their own and others' safety in all activities;
* understand the safety risks of wearing inappropriate clothing, footwear and jewellery;
* lift, carry and place equipment safely;
* respond readily to instructions and signals within established routines and follow relevant rules and codes.

Health-related exercise

In PE lessons pupils should be taught to:

* be physically active;
* engage in activities that involve the whole body, maintain flexibility and develop strength and endurance;
* adopt good posture and the correct use of the body at all times.

Planning for PE

This will support planning at all levels and includes:
* **Schemes of work** covering the whole key stage.
* **Units of work** for a term or year.
* **Lesson plans** for a class or group.

Units of work can be presented for a short intensive period of activity (eg 15 minutes daily) or as part of a cross-curricular activity (eg dance/drama across the curriculum).

Each area of activity does not need an equal share of curriculum time, provided that all areas of the PoS have been covered by the end of the key stage. At Key Stages 1 and 2 it is recommended that emphasis be placed on gymnastics, dance and games in order to create a basic repertoire of movement skills and understanding. Athletics and outdoor activities will need less time at Key Stage 1. The organisation of swimming in individual schools will be influenced by the availability of pool facilities, transport and teacher expertise. There is evidence to suggest that swimming is best learnt through short, but intensive participation, eg swimming every day for a month.

Important aspects of planning will include breadth and balance, progression, differentiation to meet individual needs, assessment and record-keeping.

Breadth and balance

Breadth and balance can be provided by a combination of:

- games/athletics, gymnastics, dance, and outdoor/adventurous activities;
- competitive and non-competitive activity;
- contact and non-contact activity;
- group, pair and individual activity;
- emphasis on developing physical skill and on tactical understanding;
- use of different teaching approaches (see below).

Fig 2: An example of a PE programme at Key Stage 1

Teachers will need to respond to local circumstances, school traditions and children's needs in planning their programme. The following is one possible framework for PE at Key Stage 1:

	Reception			Year 1			Year 2		
	Autumn	Spring	Summer	Autumn	Spring	Summer	Autumn	Spring	Summer
Gymnastics	✔ ✔[1]	✔ ✔[2]	✔ ✔	✔ ✔[2]	✔ ✔	✔ ✔	✔ ✔	✔ ✔	✔ ✔
Games/Athletics[3]	✔ ✔	✔ ✔	✔ ✔	✔ ✔	✔ ✔	✔ ✔	✔ ✔	✔ ✔	✔ ✔
Dance	✔ ✔	✔ ✔	✔	✔ ✔	✔ ✔	✔	✔ ✔	✔ ✔	✔
Outdoor Ed	✔	✔	✔ ✔	✔	✔ ✔	✔ ✔	✔	✔	✔ + swimming

✔ = represents half a term

1 = Floor gymnastics

2 = Limited apparatus

3 = Indoor if wet

N.B.

1. Aim for 3 or 4 lessons per week, if possible, to ensure breadth and balance.

2. Other activities across the curriculum can ensure some physical activity daily, eg drama, RE/drama, use of play area/frame, active playtimes, outdoor education, maths/science trails.

With whole-school planning, imagination and flexibility we can ensure children receive a balanced programme in PE.

Progression

Children develop at different rates, so rate of progress in PE will vary and may be affected by illness, accident or absence. Children who are injured or otherwise excused from PE can still participate in some aspect of the work, for example, reporting on or evaluating the progress of others, by recording activity, eg through drawing, or devising rules for a game. Children's development in PE will involve progression from:

- Dependence to independence, eg 'Can you do your movements on your own?'
- Repeating given tasks, to creating and structuring their own, eg 'Can you create your own movements?'
- Using given criteria to judge performance, to developing their own criteria for identifying a 'good' performance, eg 'Can you say or show why you think it is a good movement ?'
- Simple activities, to more complex activities and sequences, eg 'Can you add more movements?'
- Natural movement, to skilful/aesthetic performance, eg 'Can you make your movements look good?'

    The elements of progress are difficulty, and quality in the planning, performing and evaluation of physical activities. Progress in levels of difficulty can be achieved by asking for:

- Greater variety in movements within a task, eg 'Can you make different shapes?'
- Improved performance in movement, eg 'Can you show me a better shape?'
- Improved co-ordination of movements, eg 'Can you change from one shape to another?'

At Key Stage 1, PE should develop from children's free play, into more purposeful, planned and skilful activity. Much of this early movement experience will be based on repetition, to help children develop the confidence, control and body awareness which will provide a sound basis for more difficult and complex activity later.

Differentiation

Planning for PE means seeking to cater for a range of different abilities and needs. This will mean making provision for groups of children with similar needs, and for those with individual or special needs. This is a demanding task, best achieved by:

- building on the past achievements of individual pupils;
- planning to develop specific skills, knowledge and understanding;
- encouraging participation of those with physical impairment or special needs;
- providing opportunities for each child to experience success.

Strategies should include **differentiation by task**: children working through a series of activities with increasing levels of difficulty, eg catching with two hands/one hand/left hand/right hand; and **differentiation by outcome**: children engaged on a common task which allows for different levels of response, eg creating a dance to the same piece of music.

Children with special needs

Children with special needs have an entitlement to a broad and balanced PE programme relevant to those needs. The best results are achieved by matching tasks and resources to the needs of the pupils. If the task is too difficult the pupil will fail. If it is too easy the pupil will succeed with little satisfaction or skill development. Strategies that help in meeting special needs include:

• breaking down an activity into small achievable steps;
• adapting and simplifying tasks so that success can be achieved;
• presenting an activity slowly and clearly;
• demonstrating or modelling an activity;
• encouraging work with a sympathetic partner.

An effective programme will involve planning for differentiation by providing:

• a variety of resources for different levels of ability;
• a variety of grouping – individual, pairs, groups (sometimes according to ability);
• a variety of tasks, using different allocations of time, different roles and expectations.

For more on children with special needs in PE see pp115–116.

Assessment

Teachers should use the end of key stage statements as reference points for assessment in PE. There are not the levels of attainment that are common to most other foundation subjects, and it is important, therefore, for teachers to keep their own continuing assessments of pupils' progress in PE. The gathering of evidence will include observation, recording and reporting.

Observation and discussion is the most obvious way of collecting evidence in PE. Children should be encouraged to use self-assessment, and opportunities provided for them, to observe, evaluate and communicate on their own and each other's performance. Observers might be asked to look for variety, eg 'How many different ways?' or for quality, eg 'Can you pick out something good in what you see?'.

Recording of evidence over a period of time is important, so that evidence of achievement and progress is noted throughout the key stage, and not just left to the end.

Reporting should reflect the positive achievements of each child in each area of the PoS. Schools can select their own format for reporting to parents, for example, either a general comment on attainment and progress, or specific comments and levels of attainment. At the end of the key stage there is, of course, a statutory requirement to report with reference to the EKSS. Records should be kept to a minimum, so as not to be time-consuming or interfere with teaching. For more on assessment and examples of record sheets see pp101–114.

Managing the PE lesson

In organising and managing a PE lesson*, key factors such as communication, discipline, safety and equal opportunities will need consideration.

Communication
Important elements of good communication include:
• **Being prepared**: plan what is to be said, prepare the resources, be clear about the aims of the lesson, be aware of the needs of the children. Make a plan of the lesson on paper, or note key points on a small card (kept under watch strap) or in your head if you have a good memory!
• **Being clear**: stand where all can see you, emphasise key points, repeat if necessary (or check understanding by asking them to tell you). Avoid asking vague questions like 'Shall we...? Would you like to...?'; make statements instead like 'We are going to...'
• **Being simple**: use simple language; rephrase if necessary, don't talk too much (children want to move!). Use a simple signal for 'stop' and 'go'; use gestures to reinforce your message.
• **Being vivid**: vary the voice, be enthusiastic. Speak quietly sometimes (when you have full attention), project your voice sometimes, eg to praise a child across the room; put feeling into your voice.
• **Being natural**: successful PE teaching can be defined as 'grace under pressure'; being natural and relaxed is not easy when you are organising large numbers of children. Tell the children how you feel (it will help them to understand you), and try the relaxing effect of a smile or laugh.

Discipline
The management of the PE lesson begins in the classroom or in the changing room. Remind children about the rules and routines before they begin to change. Walk with care and poise to the PE area and check

*For more on class management see *Teaching Juniors* by Robert Fisher (Simon & Schuster) pp28–55.

that they are quiet and controlled before beginning to warm up. Practise the routines that make for a smooth PE lesson: keep all the children in view all the time; remind the children of the three or four basic rules that you have agreed and deal firmly with 'rule-breakers' by, eg, withdrawing them from the activity for a short period, after due warning. Be clear about the noise level you will permit; make them work in absolute silence if you think this will aid their concentration and effort. Anticipate problems by keeping actively involved in what they are doing and don't punish groups or the whole class for the misdemeanours of individuals. Try to catch them being good: praise good behaviour and effort. Remember, the lesson does not end until they have changed and are back in the classroom.

Safety

The safety of the children should be the first concern in any activity: be aware of the safety code of the school; know what to do in an emergency and identify the member(s) of staff responsible for first-aid. Check that equipment is stable and in good condition and that ground surfaces are dry, clean and free from obstacles. Walls should be free from protrusions, especially sharp metal, and ensure that there is sufficient space for the children to work in. If an accident occurs, stop whatever is going on and ask the children to sit quietly. If necessary, ask a child to fetch another adult. The first rule of first-aid is: if in doubt, don't. Always follow the accident procedures of the school.

Equal opportunities

Every child has an entitlement to PE. This means that children should not be denied PE as a punishment, although they may be withdrawn from an activity during the lesson if their behaviour is dangerous, or they are denying opportunities for others. All children should be allowed access to the activities of the lesson, and have experience of handling apparatus. Avoid situations which create gender differentiation or stereotyping, such as boys' groups and girls' groups. Try not to use sexist or gender-related language, such as 'Boys march like soldiers. Girls dance like ballet dancers'. Boys and girls should have access to all games, and to all kinds of equipment.

Just as we avoid gender bias, we should also beware of cultural or racial bias. Much can be learnt from the sports and physical activities practised in differing ethnic and cultural groups. PE has an important role to play in every society; our physical activity helps us to define who we are. So what teaching strategies should we use?

Teaching approaches and learning opportunities

Children have different needs and abilities, but all need the opportunity to plan, perform and review their physical activities. There is no one right way to teach PE. To achieve success we need to use different teaching approaches to match the needs of different activities, individual children and changing circumstances. The following teaching strategies can be adapted to help children explore, invent, plan, perform, enjoy, observe and review their actions – to experience **active PE**.

• **Experimenting**: through providing apparatus or equipment for children to play freely, discover their abilities and how to use their expressive physical qualities. For very young children, such play is essential for early development. Older children also need these opportunities when introduced to new activities, or when confidence is lacking. Children with special needs may benefit from more extended opportunities for experimental play.

• **Problem-solving**: through giving children problems to investigate, for example: How many different ways can you move along (or across) a bench? Can you make different shapes with your body? How can you move through these hoops without touching them?

• **Task-setting**: through a specific task being set by the teacher or by the children, for example: Balance on two hands and one foot; Jump with a big stretch before landing; Take your weight on your hands and kick up one/both feet.

• **Skill-teaching**: through a skill being taught by means of exposition or demonstration, or a combination of both ('show and tell'). Breaking the skill down into short steps can be helpful; also rehearsing what you are about to do, talking through what you are showing, and inviting or asking questions. This also reflects the old teaching strategy of 'tell 'em before they do it, tell 'em while they are doing it, and tell 'em after they have done it.'

After a short period of experimentation, most children will benefit from a degree of skill teaching. Children should also be encouraged to invent new ideas or movements for others to try, to share skills with each other and learn to appreciate each other's efforts. A balance between these approaches will help to ensure that all children are active and achieve success at their own level.

PE links across the curriculum

Fig 3: PE: a cross-curricular perspective

PE has important contributions to make across the curriculum: to cross-curricular skills such as communication and problem-solving; to cross-curricular themes such as health education, environmental and social education; and to common themes in all areas of the curriculum. The following chart shows some of the cross-curricular perspectives of PE:

HEALTH EDUCATION
(Health-related exercise)
- Posture: sitting, standing, lying
- Poise
- Hygiene
- Body changes
- Diet/sleep/rest
- Safety

PERSONAL/SOCIAL EDUCATION
(Education for Citizenship)
- Co-operation/self-discipline/self-reliance
- Empathy, appreciation, sensitivity
- Self-image, confidence
- Success/failure
- Handling competition

MATHEMATICS
(AT 1, 2, 3, 4)
- Measurement, pattern/shape, space, estimation, travel and time, number, angles
- Maths language: big/small, high/low, straight/curved

SCIENCE (AT 2, 41ii)
- Shape in animals, plants, machines, buildings
- Movement in the above, people, vehicles
- Growth in plants, animals, human body
- Floating/sinking/water

MYSELF SHAPE + SPACE MOVEMENT TRAVEL TIME

ANIMALS

OUR BODIES   COMMUNI-CATION

KEEPING HEALTHY

PHYSICAL EDUCATION
gymnastics, dance, games, athletics, swimming, outdoor education

MOODS + FEELINGS

SAFETY   LOCAL ENVIRONMENT

HOMES WEATHER JOURNEYS

ENGLISH (AT 1, 3)
- Vocabulary of movement/games, etc
- Listening, talking, writing, describing, discussing performance. Stop/go, on/off, over/under/through/round/between/long/thin/narrow/wide/stretch/extend/fast/slow, etc
(Link story, rhyme, poetry)

HISTORY/GEOGRAPHY
- Environmental education
- Outdoor education
- Representing past in movement and dance
- Dances in different countries/cultures

TECHNOLOGY (AT 1, 2, 4)
- Handling information - lists, charts, database
- Shapes: rolling, turning, rigid, fixed
- Bridges/structures, tables/chairs
- Friction/sliding/pulling/pushing
- Use of calculator, stop watch, measures
- IT Simple programmes/ database
- Flight/movement of apparatus/self

DRAMA MUSIC ART
(Aesthetic education)
- Communication, relationships, moods, feelings
- Appreciation of space, form, rhythm

Active in body and mind

What we are developing and assessing in PE is an important aspect of a child's development – that of physical intelligence. It is part of the problem-solving, and expressive or creative capacity of human life. Carrying out a dance sequence or hitting a tennis ball are not problems in a logical or linguistic sense; they are problems demanding physical intelligence, involving use of both mind and body. Even the simplest of human actions can involve skill and grace and can present real physical challenge. The exhiliration of success, the widening range of physical skill and a growing awareness of one's own body and self – all these and more can be provided by PE. In writing about the need to combine body and mind in tennis, Tim Gallwey (1976) observed: 'To return an average serve, you have about a second to do this. To hit the ball at all is remarkable and yet not uncommon. The truth is that everyone who inhabits a human body possesses a remarkable creation'. It is to help our children make the most of their 'remarkable creation' that we seek to make the most out of their physical education lessons, to fulfil the potential of an active body and mind. As one child observed after a PE lesson: 'I didn't know I can do it until I done it. I wonder if I can do something I can't do next time?'

Gymnastics

'I am so happy I could jump over myself!'
(six year-old returning from a PE lesson)

Young children love physical activity. If they have been physically fit and active in their early years they will already have had experience of basic gymnastic actions such as travelling, turning, rolling, jumping, balancing, swinging, and climbing on apparatus.

What gymnastics in school should provide is experience of many ways of performing these basic actions. PE lessons should give children opportunities to practise, adapt, and improve control of their individual actions. As they become more physically skilled and confident they should be given opportunities to link together a series of actions, both on the floor and on apparatus, and be encouraged to repeat them. They should also be taught as part of the programme to carry and position simple apparatus using correct lifting techniques. This section on gymnastics provides a guide to the following:

- What to teach – gymnastics in the National Curriculum.
- Lesson planning.
- Skill development.
- travelling (and use of space);
- body shape;
- supporting body weight;
- transfer of weight;
- jumping (flight).

What to teach
gymnastics in the National Curriculum

'Gymnastic activities focus on the body. They are concerned with acquiring control, co-ordination and versatility in the use of the body, and responding to challenges.'
(National Curriculum PE Working Group for Interim Report, 1991)

The Statements of Attainment in the National Curriculum say that at the end of Key Stage 1, by the age of seven years, pupils should be able to:

- plan and perform safely a range of simple activities and linked movements in response to given tasks and stimuli;

- practise and improve their performance;
- describe what they and others are doing;
- recognise the effects of physical activities on their bodies;
- begin to co-operate and work with others.
  (PE in the National Curriculum, 1992)

The Programmes of Study say that pupils should experience ways of performing the actions of:

■ travelling
■ balancing
■ turning
■ swinging
■ rolling
■ climbing
■ jumping
■ bearing weight on hands.

The following units of work or themes aim to cover the Statements of Attainment and Programmes of Study: Travelling (and use of space); Body shape; Supporting body weight; Transferring weight; Jumping (flight). Within each theme attention should be given to different aspects of movement, and in particular to:

- **Pathways**: movements using a variety of straight and curved pathways on the floor.
- **Levels**: movements in relation to the floor, using low, medium or high areas of space.
- **Directions**: exploring different directions; forwards, backwards, sideways and up and down.
- **Linking movements** together: movements in which pupils build up sequences on and off the apparatus (to be included to add variety, challenge and develop the main themes in later stages towards the end of KS1).

'Let me do it again. I think I can do it better' *(five year-old)*.
All improvements in physical skill depend on practice, and on being mindful about what is being done. Children need opportunities to repeat the movements they know and the movements they are learning, to help them improve physical skills and control. They also need encouragement to think about their actions, and to develop ideas and understanding about the movements they make.

Lesson planning

'I change into PE clothes at break or lunchtime, so that I'm ready for the busiest part of the lesson – getting the children changed!'

(student teacher).

Preparing for the PE lesson

The PE lesson begins in the classroom; not the gymnastics of course, but preparation for what in the past was called 'gym'. Time can be taken to review key points from the last lesson. Reminders can be given about how to walk to the hall or PE location. In planning the lesson look for links with classwork . Think about the apparatus required: is it spaced conveniently around the edge of the hall for later moving and use?

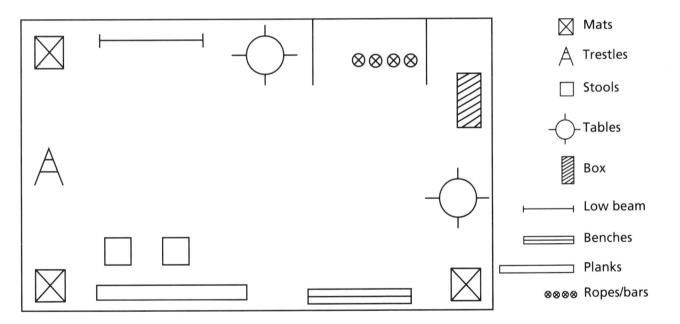

Fig 4: Diagram showing PE apparatus around a hall (with key)

One way to prepare is to be changed yourself – at least by wearing PE shoes. The lesson begins when changing starts, and ends when changing finishes. What children change out of and into is a matter of school policy, but it does not have to be an individual activity; they can change in pairs to help each other. Try timing them to speed them up: can they improve their personal best for both children in a pair being ready?

Organising the apparatus

When apparatus is used you will need to consider the children's age, and their ability to handle the equipment. You will need to link your use of the apparatus with previous groups, or the next group in the hall. It is important for children to begin to handle and move the apparatus (planks, stools, mats, forms, etc) at an early age providing it is safe and they are physically able to do so. (For advice on light, adaptable equipment see Resources p119.) Part of PE is learning about the apparatus or equipment: what each piece is called, how it is used and how it may be moved and fixed for safety.

Apparatus should be moved by children as part of the lesson, starting with mats, planks, benches, and/or low tables. Spending time on handling the apparatus in the early stages will pay dividends later. The following are some points to remember:

- use four children as the handling group for each piece of apparatus;
- teach a good lifting position, with straight backs, and bent knees;
- teach children to lift apparatus into position; don't drag apparatus or mats across the floor;
- praise and show good practice every lesson (use a good group to demonstrate);
- move apparatus one or two pieces at a time (handled by one or two groups);
- move more apparatus at a time as competence grows (eg by half the class at a time);
- move apparatus from/to sides of the hall to designated positions for ease and speed of access;
- discuss in the classroom the safe carrying of apparatus, and other heavy loads;
- discuss the position of apparatus in class (eg by using a chart on the wall).

The diagrams opposite show the importance of placement of mats and apparatus to allow a variety of approaches to and landings from apparatus.

Fig 5 : Arranging the apparatus – three models using mats, benches and box-tops

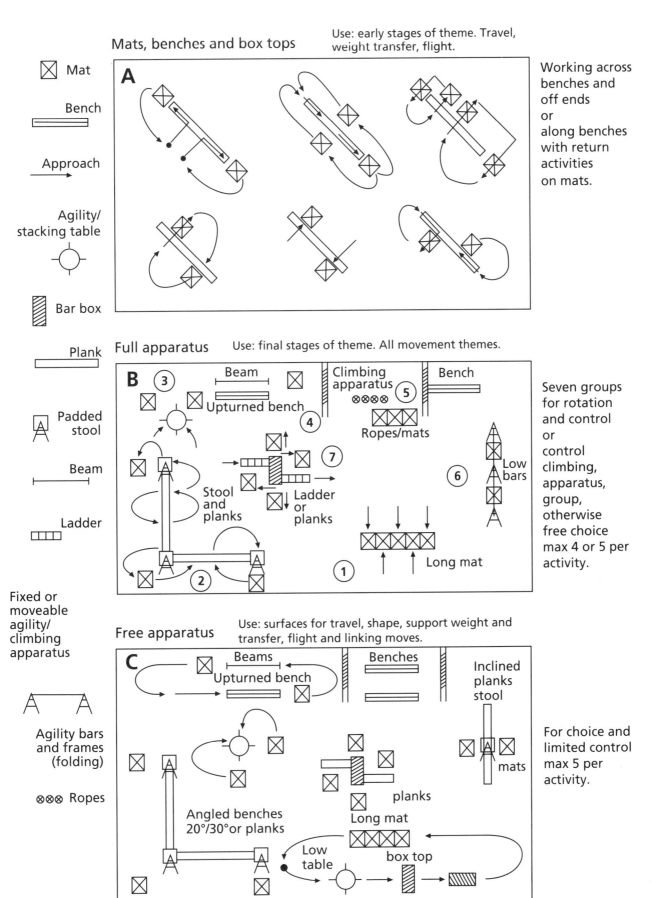

Planning a lesson

The length of the lesson will vary to suit the age of the children. A typical lesson might last from 15–20 minutes for four to five year-olds, to 20–30 minutes for six to seven year-olds. A plan for a lesson might be:

1. **Introduction/warm up** (2–3 minutes): to prepare body for later activity.
2. **Floorwork** (7–10 minutes): a theme explored and developed through tasks set by teacher.
3. **Apparatus work** (8–12 minutes): a theme developed on small or large equipment.
4. **Conclusion** (2–3 minutes): a quiet, controlled activity to calm and relax.

It is not necessary for there to be floorwork and apparatus work for each lesson; an alternative model might be, for example, on consecutive days, warm-up + floorwork + ending, then warm-up (remember yesterday's floorwork)+ develop on apparatus + ending.

Fig 6: Use apparatus to gain maximum activity.

Jumping and landing (flight)

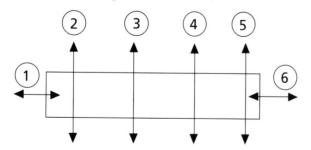

3+ children ACTIVE on box and 3 mats

Supporting Weight (balance)

4 children showing position of balance on floor and apparatus

Transfer of weight (hands-feet)

Pathways/use of space

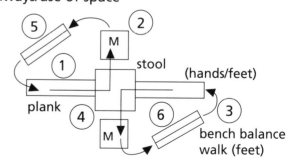

Each lesson should have a theme through which gymnastic skills can be explored and developed. The following are five themes, each of which could form the basis of a series of lessons or unit of work in PE.

Themes for skill development

The themes are explored with a list of developing activities which contain enough basic material for you to plan several lessons. Each theme follows the warm up/floorwork/apparatus/conclusion pattern recommended earlier. Focus on one or two activities from each section in each lesson. Children will respond to tasks and activities at their own level: try to vary and add tasks appropriate to the needs and abilities of individual children.

Travelling (and use of space)

Travelling involving use of space involves different ways of moving using the feet, or using hands and feet, or large parts of the body like tummy or bottom. Select from the following activities to create lessons with warm-up, floorwork, apparatus work and conclusion on the theme of travelling.

Warm up

The following are some warm-up activities emphasising travelling and use of space:

(a)

- Quiet walking/jogging/running in different directions; listen for stop signal. Make sure nobody is near you.
- Move as above into space to make a small/big/other shape.
- Find different ways to travel in space on your feet and stop in animal/plant/machine shape (a).
- Skip/hop/jump freely; stop on signal in action photograph.
- Move in different ways forwards/backwards/sideways, keeping a space around you.
- Move in different ways up/down/turning, with nobody near you.
- Move on hands and feet forwards/backwards/sideways/turning (b).

(b)

- Move on other body parts keeping tummy/bottom/one foot held high.
- Move quietly/lightly/smoothly/quickly. Freeze on signal.
- Move under/through/round half class, who freeze in a set shape. Change over.

Floorwork

The following activities involve travel and use of floor space:

- Travelling on hands and feet, make stretching and curling shapes; move in different directions (c). **(c)**

- Keeping hands on the floor, move feet to make small and big shapes.
- Keeping feet on the floor, move hands to make small and big shapes.
- Travel, using half or three-quarters of your body; move into spaces without touching others.
- Show different ways to jump – try jumping as high or as far as you can.
- Run three or four steps, then jump to land on two feet; be still, then try again.

(d)

- Curl up, hold knees, rock forwards/backwards/sideways(d).
- Practise rocking/rolling with body curled and then stretched.
- Roll on floor slowly/smoothly/quietly. Roll in different ways and directions.
- Travel in different ways, eg sliding/rolling, on large body parts, eg tummy, bottom.

Small apparatus

At a later stage, use of small apparatus such as beanbags, hoops or ropes can add variety to floorwork. The apparatus chosen can be used as a) a point of contact; b) an object to avoid; c) an object to reach.

The following are some activities with small apparatus that can help develop gymnastic skills:

(e)

- Jumping over, around, in and out of a hoop or rope shape.
- Keeping hands on a beanbag on the floor, walk your feet in different directions (e).
- Keeping your feet inside a hoop on the ground, how far can you reach on your hands?
- Walk forwards/backwards/sideways along a rope placed on the floor.
- Jump over two beanbags placed 50 cm apart. Increase this distance if successful (f).
- Ask the children to invent more actions using the above activities with small apparatus as starting points.

(f)

Large apparatus

Start with simple layouts, using, for example, mats, benches and low, flat surfaces (see p23).

The following are some activities using large apparatus to develop travelling skills in gymnastics:

- Find ways to climb on or off apparatus slowly, without touching other children.
- Climb on or off the apparatus from another place, moving slowly/quietly/lightly (g).
- Find a safe place on the apparatus to be small or big, and change shape on signal.
- Move in spaces under/round or through/over the apparatus – then try without touching the floor!

(g)

(h)

• Jump on, climb off the apparatus slowly from the same or a different place forwards/backwards/sideways.
• Move freely all over your apparatus without stopping, moving over/along/up/down/through (h).
• Travel on/off/under/over/along/across the apparatus, using hands and feet (encourage a variety of approaches).
• Climb on to the apparatus slowly, jump off with a spring; jump on with a spring, climb off slowly.

Conclusion

These end-of-the-lesson activities are best introduced after the apparatus has been returned to its place. They are intended to calm and relax the body after strenuous activity:

• Walk quietly/slowly/lightly into a space, and curl up like a small animal.
• Practice a movement you learned or liked today.
• Move smoothly into spaces, and stop on signal in set shape (link to classwork).
• Lie still: what can you hear? Stretch/curl/stretch and relax.
• From lying position, rock or roll to a new position; be still.
• Move from a curl to stretch position. Link with night and day, or plant growth, etc.

Body shape

There are two kinds of body shape actions that children need to practise and think about: the first emphasises movement in curling and stretching, and involves change in the extension of body shape; the second emphasises twisting and turning, and involves a change of direction in body shape.

Select from the following activities to create lessons with warm-up, apparatus work and conclusion on the theme of body shape.

Warm up

The following are some warm-up activities emphasising body shape:

• Walk to a space, stop: on given signal make a curled/stretched/long/ wide shape.
• Run without touching others: stop in a curl (or stretch) position.
• Jump on the spot, swing arms up to make a stretched/wide/long shape.
• Jump on the spot and stop in a crouched position (like a Jack-in-the-box).
• Move on hands and feet, stop in a space and make the shape of ... (something linked with a story or classwork).

Floorwork

The following activities involve body shapes using the floor:

(i)

(j)

- Lie down; curl your body; stretch your body; rock on to different parts of the body.
- Lie with weight on your back. Use your legs to make different shapes and angles. With arms straight, take your weight on your hands and kick up legs (i).
- Curl up from the floor and stretch out to balance your body on your feet, hands and feet or other part of the body.
- Sit with weight on bottom; curl/stretch/twist your tummy, hip or other part of the body (j).
- Run three or four steps then jump to a wide, long or twisted shape.
- Jump, twist your body, land, and be still.
- Jump, twist, land, add a roll and be still.
- Run, jump, land, curl (or stretch) and be still.
- Run, jump, land, twist or turn your body and be still.

Small apparatus

Many of the above activities can be adapted for use with small apparatus as: a) a point of contact; b) an object to avoid; c) an object to reach.

Large apparatus

Start with simple layouts, using, for example, mats, benches and low, flat surfaces (see p23).

The following are some activities using large apparatus to develop body shape in gymnastics:

(k)

- Find different ways to contact apparatus in curled or stretched position (k).
- Climb on apparatus to find an empty space, curl for three seconds, then stretch.
- Climb on apparatus as before; curl, then stretch, with part of your body taking weight on the floor.
- Jump from apparatus, stretched long and wide. Bend knees on landing and be still.
- Move off apparatus slowly on any body part, stretch and be still.
- Move over/along/under/around apparatus in curl or stretch position.
- Move on apparatus as above, in curl and stretch positions alternately, and stop on signal.
- Hang or balance upside down from apparatus, near the floor, using the apparatus for support.
- Move freely on apparatus; freeze in special shape on teacher's command and curl/stretch/twist/go upside down/lift a part of your body as high as you can.

(l)

Many of the previous activities can be adpated to use a) with a partner moving together or apart (l); b) lifting body parts as high as you can, eg hands, feet, tummy, knees (m).

(m)

Conclusion

The following activities can bring a lesson on body shape to a calm and relaxed ending:

- Practise any shapes you enjoy. Can you join two together?
- Make your body into the shape of something you can see near you, then relax onto the floor.
- Lie still, long and thin, listen to ... (sound), roll and curl up and rest.
- Can you make a bridge shape (or other shape from classwork), then slowly collapse your bridge?

Supporting body weight

Supporting body weight means holding the weight of the body still using different parts of the body as a basis, particularly the hands and feet. Bodies are quite heavy; do your children know how much they weigh? What parts of their body can they use to support their body weight?

The following are some activities that can be used to create lessons with warm up, apparatus work and conclusion, on the theme of supporting body weight.

Warm up

The following are some warm-up activities emphasising support of body weight:

- Practise walking or jogging, stop on different body parts, eg feet, hands and feet, knees, bottom.
- Move in zig-zag directions on feet or hands and feet.
- Running or jumping on spot, try to tuck knees up high.
- Jump, and when you land, make patterns on the floor with your feet.
- Move with feet together by jumping. Try other ways to move with feet together.
- Make patterns with your feet on the floor as you run/hop/skip.
- Practise starting and stopping on a given signal; bend knees as you run and keep your hips low when you stop (n).
- Jump to land on one, and then two, feet.
- Take two or three steps, jump, and land lightly; be still.

(n)

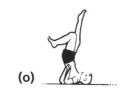

(o)

(p)

Floorwork

The following activities involve support of body weight using the floor:

- Stand tall, lower your body to sit, kneel, or lie down.
- Balance on any parts of your body; be still for a count of ... seconds.
- Count to five or more. How many of your body parts can you make touch the floor?
- Take weight on knees/shoulders/hip/bottom/tummy (o).
- Take weight on hands or hands and feet/elbows/knees/other (p).
- Curl up, roll on to a new part of your body, stand and stretch tall.
- Balance on parts of your body and hold your tummy, feet or other part, high.
- Take your weight on your hands and crouch, keeping your arms straight, and bounce your feet up in the air.
- Take your weight on hands and feet, face the floor, ceiling or walls, and stretch your body.
- Crouch- or bunny-jump, hands to feet like rabbits, with bottoms up.
- Make high or low bridges with different parts of your body.

Small apparatus

The following are some activities with small apparatus involving support of body weight using beanbags:

- Keeping one or both feet on the floor, try to touch the beanbag with different body parts: heel, toe, hand, wrist, elbow, back, shoulder, knee, forehead, etc (q).

(q)

- Balance on one part of the body while touching the bag on a different part. (This task can be made more challenging by increasing the distance of the bag from the body.)
- Balance on a bag with feet, tummy, bottom, knees or shoulders.
- Ropes in parallel or made into shapes can be used in the above activities.
- Quoits and small hoops can also add interest and challenge in the same way.

Large apparatus

Start with simple layouts, using, for example, mats, benches and low, flat surfaces (see p23). The following are some activities using large apparatus to develop support of body weight in gymnastics:

- Climb on to apparatus slowly, find a space, hold tight and be still.

- Move forwards/backwards/sideways into a space, and be still.
- Climb on to apparatus as above; on a given signal move on to different parts of your body; move off apparatus slowly, feet first, hands first, knees first, or any other way that you can.

(r)

- Balance or hang on hands and feet, bottom, back, backs of legs, or another part of your body (r).
- Hang or balance on the apparatus, supported by the floor and the apparatus.
- On signal, stop in hanging or balance position.
- Move up/along/over apparatus as above, but finish in a balance position on floor, touching apparatus (s).

(s)

- Move off the apparatus forwards/sideways/backwards.
- Move off the apparatus slowly/with a spring.
- Combine the last two moves as a separate movement.

Conclusion

The following activities can bring a lesson on support of body weight to a calm and relaxed ending:

- Practise a favourite floor balance.
- Curl up small, spring out into a stretch position, then curl up small again.
- With weight on hands, do bunnyhops in a small space.
- Lying on back, listen to breathing, roll on to front, tuck up ready and stand.

Transfer of weight

Transfer of weight is a development of the theme of travelling, when the part of the body supporting the body weight is changed; for example, moving weight from one part to another, such as from feet to hands; or transferring weight on to the same part, such as hopping on the same foot.

The following are some activities that can be used to create lessons with warm-up, floorwork, apparatus work and conclusion, on the theme of transfer of weight.

Warm up

The following are some warm-up activities emphasising transfer of body weight:

- Walking in all directions fast/slowly/heavily/lightly/quietly.
- Walk like a ... (choose an animal or other topic from classwork).
- Walk forwards and backwards; walk in different ways, eg marching to a beat.
- Jogging, practise dodging and swerving round other children: stop on given signal. No touching!

- Run, and stop on a signal; turn, run in a new direction into a space.
- Move about the hall on hands and feet, forwards/backwards/sideways.
- Jump about the hall; jump big/small/high/low/long/over the moon?
- Jump into spaces on one/two feet; from two feet to one foot; from one foot to two feet.
- Follow a partner on any of the above activities.

Floorwork

During these activities, ask frequent questions: 'Can you feel the floor with your body?' 'What part of your body is touching the floor now?' The following activities involve support of body weight using the floor:

- Lie on the floor. Rock on your back/tummy/side to bottom/feet.
  - Curl up small; roll over into another curled shape on the floor.
  - Stretch up high and move to a low, stretched shape, and return to a curl shape each time (t).

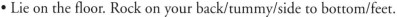

(t)

- Curl up small; stretch out into different wide/long/tall positions.
- Balance in a stretch shape; curl on to a different body part.
- Jump on the spot making different patterns of steps.
- With arms straight, kick up legs and come down on a new spot.
  - Take your weight on your hands, and bring feet down one/two at a time, legs straight or bent.
  - Find ways to balance; move/roll to a balance, high or low (u).

(u)

Small apparatus

The following are some activities with small apparatus involving support of body weight using beanbags or hoops.

Beanbags
- Jumping over beanbags in different directions.
- Hopping over a beanbag to land on one foot or two feet.
- Hopping over a beanbag as above, but with a twist; be still on landing.
- Using two or more beanbags, jump or hop over them, or move in and out in different directions. Vary the number of beanbags and the distance between them.

Hoops
- Use hands and feet to move over/in and out/around a hoop.
- Move on to different body parts inside a hoop.
- With hoop(s) on the ground, make a pattern of jumps in/out, over/around.
- Find ways to pass through a hoop held vertically in front of you. Older children may try with hoops raised to different levels.

Large apparatus

Start with simple layouts, using, for example, mats, benches and low, flat surfaces (see p23). The following are some activities using large apparatus to develop transfer of body weight in gymnastics:

- Transfer some of the floor tasks for use on the apparatus.
- Find ways to move along/across/over/under/round the apparatus.
- Find a safe place and be still. What part of your body is touching the apparatus?
- Climb on the apparatus slowly; move on to a different part of your body, and then another part.

  - Jump on the apparatus, hang/rest on hands/feet, tummy, back or knees.
  - Get on/off the apparatus slowly: forwards/backwards/sideways (v).

(v)

- Get on/off the apparatus hands first/feet first, with a roll/turn.
- Find ways to rock/roll/turn/twist along/across the apparatus (w).

(w)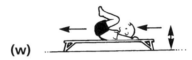

Remind children that they should ask for support or help if they need it when using the apparatus.

Conclusion

The following activities can bring a lesson on transfer of body weight to a calm and relaxed ending:

  - Find ways to curl, rock/roll on a mat (one mat between two).

(x)

- Rock from shoulders to bottom, to crouch on feet (x).
- Teach or practise the forward roll on a mat: place hands on floor just in front of feet, fingers forward; tuck chin down on chest and look back between legs; keep tucked up like a ball; push forward from two feet to shoulders/bottom; crouch on feet (y).

(y)

NB this is a basic gymnastic movement and important as a safety skill. Some children find it hard and will need teacher and partner help.

- Transfer weight from feet (standing), to bottom (sitting), to back, etc (lying).

• Lie on floor; lift and feel the heavy weight of each part of the body, eg arms, feet, bottom, etc; lower quietly.

Jumping (flight)

This theme should be introduced towards the end of Key Stage 1, when children are confident in a range of gymnastic activities. It is important when jumping to coach deep landing, with feet together, knees bent, hips bent, especially when jumping for height or from apparatus.

The following are some activities that can be used to create lessons with warm up, apparatus work and conclusion, on the theme of jumping and flight.

Warm up
The following are some warm-up activities emphasising jumping:

• Travel on different parts of your body, feet and hands, and feet/hands to feet.
• With feet together, jump in different directions.
• Run and jump as far or as high as you can.
• Jump high and lift your arms/knees/feet/heels/head as high as possible.
• Crouch, and on signal, spring up high (Jack-in-a-box).
• Jump, twisting in the air to land in a tucked or stretched position.
• Run and jump: land with feet together or apart; land on one or two feet.
• Run, kick up high (as in scissor-jump) and land one foot at a time.

Floorwork and small apparatus
The following activities involve developing jumping skills using floor, and small apparatus such as hoops:

(z)

(aa)

• Take weight on your hands; kick up one/both feet (z).
• Take weight on hands, as above. Keep bottom up high, bring legs down in a new place.
• Jump into/over/around a hoop or rope on the floor (aa).
• Jump from one hoop to another.
• Jump on the spot to make various shapes in the air.
• Make a pattern of jumps on the spot.
• Join two or three jumps together to cover as much space as possible.
• Jump, by springing from one foot to another, or from two feet to one foot, or from one foot to two feet.
• Can you spring from one to another body part (eg hands to feet, knees to bottom or feet, head and hands to feet)?
• Move like an animal that springs (shows flight) from the ground, eg kangaroo, horse, frog.

Note: Do not use a crash mat for jumping off large apparatus unless for safety reasons. It is better to use thick landing mats where possible, to encourage controlled landings.

Large apparatus

Start with simple layouts, using, for example, mats, benches and low, flat surfaces (see p23). The following are some activities using large apparatus to develop jumping skills:

* Find different places to jump on/over your apparatus.
* Find different places to jump from the apparatus (deep landing) (bb).

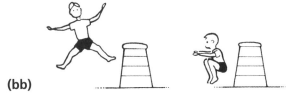

(bb)

* Jump from the apparatus with a twist in the air.
* Jump from the apparatus to stretch and reach high, with a deep landing.
* Jump from the apparatus with feet together/apart, then make a deep landing.
* Travel on the apparatus with feet apart/together, then make a deep landing.
* Hands on low apparatus, kick one or two legs as you jump to land on the the floor.
* Hang/swing on two ropes or one rope, and jump to land with feet on mat or bench.

Conclusion

The following activities can bring a lesson on jumping to a calm and relaxed ending:

* Practise a sequence of jumps in a small space.
* Spring from hands to feet (bunnyhops) in different directions.
* Standing jumps to and from a line. How far can you jump?
* Lying on your back, raise different parts high, eg legs, tummy, knees.
* Lying on your back, bend your knees, shut your eyes and listen to your breathing: can you hear other sounds?

Sample lesson plans in gymnastics for Key Stage 1

The chart overleaf offers six sample lessons in gymnastics on the theme of Travelling (or use of space).

Fig 7: Six sample lessons
in gymnastics

		1	2	3	4	5	6
WARM-UP		a) Walk/jog b) As above, move to space, make animal shape	a) Repeat 1 b b) Jogging/walking. Freeze in tuck/stretch	a) Repeat 2 b. b) Different ways to travel on feet, stop in animal shape.	a) Repeat 3 b. b) Skip/hop/jump. Freeze in space. No-one near you.	a) Repeat 4 b. b) Move about hall freely to show twisting/turning movements.	a) Repeat 5 b. b) Move on differnt body parts with tummy, seat, knees.
FLOORWORK		c) Move in different directions on hands and feet. d) Hands on floor, spread feet in different places for small and big shapes.	c) Repeat 1 d d) Feet still, move hands omn floor near and far to make curl/stretch twisted shapes.	c) Repeat 2 d. d) Move on 1/2/3/4 body parts. Move to a space and freeze in action.	c) Repeat 3 d d) JUmping use 1/2 feet. Keep space around you. Jump high/long.	c) Repeat 4 d. d) Run 3 or 4 steps, jump land and still. (Bend at hips and knees.)	c) Repeat 5 d. d) Move on big body parts, rocking, rolling, sliding, gliding. Move away from each other to sides of the hall.
APPARATUS		**Mats only** e) Correct carry in 4s. f) Move along/ across/around mat on feet/hands and feet without touching anyone. g) Move across mat stretched/curled forwards, backwards, sideways.	**Mats only** e) Repeat 1 e,g. f) Travel across mat using hands and feet. g) Move along/across mat on big body parts, (eg. sliding, rocking, rolling).	**Mats and benches** e) Correct carry in 4s. Straight backs! f) Free movement. Find different ways to get on/off apparatus - no touching anyone. g) Move along/across bench on hands and feet. Jumps on to mat to be still. (Bend hips/knees).	**Mats and benches** e) Repeat 4 e. 4 groups at once. f) Repeat 3 g. g) Get on with a jump. Move along/over bench, feet only, forwards/ backwards/sideways. Get off slowly, use different body parts.	**Simple flat surfaces** (App. C) e) Be precise about apparatus handling. 2 groups handle at a time. f) Find ways to climb on/off slowly, freely without touching anyone. 'Stop' in space. Hold tight. g) Find a safe space to be small/big. Move to a new space on signal.	**Simple flat surfaces** (App. C) e) 2 groups to handle at a time. f) Repeat 5 g. g) Move along/across using large body parts sliding, pushing, curling and rolling. Use mat and floor space not apparatus.
CONCLUSION		2 groups a time h) Return mats. Praise good carriers! Good lifting habits! i) In quiet, space out! Make two shapes you enjoyed today.	4 groups a time h) Return mats to two separate places. i) Move quietly/silently curl up small, stretch to greet morning!	2 groups a time h) Return apparatus (quietest group?). i) Game, Statues. Use music/percussion to inspire/guide actions.	h) 4 groups a time to return apparatus. i) Travel in two different ways. On signal stop to lie long, wide or stand high/low. (Maths shapes.)	h) Apparatus returned carefully. (Lots of praise/encourage) i) Game. 'Teacher Says' or 'Do this, do that'. (No-one drops out)	h) Apparatus returning. No speaking. Silent communication!! i) Hibernation. Curled tight (Winter). Uncurl and grow taller (Spring).Blossom and stretch (Summer).

For Resources for gymnastics see p119.

Dance

> Round and round the apples of gold,
> Round and round dance we,
> Thus do we dance from the days of old,
> About the enchanted tree;
> While the spring is green, or the stream shall flow
> Or the wind shall stir the sea!
>
> *(Pindar c500 BC)*

Dance is an art form known to all cultures and can be used to communicate feelings and stories through rhythms and patterns of movement that are both disciplined and spontaneous. Children should experience many kinds of dance, from creative dance to folk or country dance; dance can contribute to physical development, rhythmic sense and aesthetic awareness, and through dance children can gain a satisfaction not to be found in any other activity.

Many infant teachers have relied on taped radio programmes such as *Let's move* and *Time to Move* for their dance and movement lessons. These provide a rich source of music, creative movement and follow-up activities and allow the teacher to stop the tape to give extra help, for example 'Tuck your head in to make a very small shape', or to focus on good effort: 'Look at the way John is stretching his fingers'. But a taped programme cannot match the children's responses, or relate to class themes. There is a need for teachers to create, teach and develop their own materials. This section on dance provides a guide to the following:

- What to teach – dance in the National Curriculum.
- Lesson planning.
- Resources.

What to teach — dance in the National Curriculum

The National Curriculum for dance at Key Stage 1 says that pupils should:

- experience and develop control, co-ordination, balance, poise and elevation in basic actions including travelling, jumping, turning, gesture and stillness;
- explore contrasts of speed, tension, continuity, shape, size, direction and level and describe what they have done;
- experience working with a range and variety of contrasting stimuli, including music;
- be given opportunities to explore moods and feelings through spontaneous responses and through structured tasks;

- be helped to develop rhythmic responses;
- experience, and be guided towards, making dances with clear beginnings, middles and ends.
(Stage 1 Programmes of Study, 1992)

Teachers need to plan units of work for dance that include activities which focus on:

- The body (parts of the body and body shapes).
- Actions (elements of movement).
- Dance (moving in patterns of rhythm and in relationship to others).

Lesson planning

Lesson plans for dance may include these elements:

- **Warm up**: introductory activity (2–3 minutes) (pp39–40).
- **Movement ideas**: developing awareness of the body and of actions (8–10 minutes) (pp40–41).
- **Dance theme**: creating a simple dance, exploring body/movement ideas (10–15 minutes) (pp48–60).
- **Conclusion**: to relax pupils and provide opportunites for reflection (1–2 minutes) (p61).

In planning lessons in dance keep in mind the following:

- Be prepared – have resources ready beforehand (see Resources pp119–121) .
- Link with other areas of the curriculum (see Cross-curricular links p17).
- Time lessons to the concentration-span of children, eg 20 minutes' activity for five year-olds, 30 minutes for seven year-olds, with a brisk ten minutes outside in cold weather.
- Encourage children to plan what they are going to do, practice what they are to perform, and evaluate or describe what they have done.
- Ensure a clear signal, eg clap or tambour, for stopping and starting.
- Use praise and allow demonstration to foster good effort and performance.
- Remember health, care and safety points.

Remember to make teaching:

A ctive	promoting an active and healthy lifestyle through dance.
C o-operative	working with and taking care of others through dance.
T houghtful	encouraging a thoughtful approach to dance.
I nventive	fostering a creative response to movement.
V aried	developing a variety of skills in dance.
E njoyable	enjoying dance activities in PE.

Warm-up activities

The following are some activities to encourage children to move freely, involving travel and the encouragement of body awareness:

On the spot

- Each child finds a space.
- At signal, children walk, jog or run on the spot.
- At signal, children hop on the spot. Try changing legs.
- As teacher counts or beats to ten, children see how many different things they can do without moving from their spot.
- Ask them to think of how many parts of the body they can move, bend, stretch, twist, turn, move fast/slow, high/low. Ready, steady, go (start counting). How many different actions?

Shadow punching/kicking

- On the spot swing arms out all the way round, making sure you can't touch anybody!
- Punch the air all round you, high/low, fast/slow, left/right, etc.
- Kick the air all around you, high/low, fast/slow, left/right, etc.
- Punch and kick at the same time, without falling over.
- Wind down by doing the above in slow motion.

Heads and shoulders, knees and toes

Say the action rhyme, first touching each part of the body as it is mentioned, then shaking each part as it is mentioned. Add different actions and parts of the body to the rhythm of the rhyme.

Heads and shoulders, knees and toes,
Knees and toes, knees and toes,
Heads and shoulders, knees and toes,
We all turn round together.

The place game

- Each child finds a space, and tries to memorise the spot (look for marks on floor, nearness to doors, windows, etc). Teacher explains the rules.
- At given signal children may move anywhere in room (no one must touch anyone else).
- Teacher counts or beats to ten (or to 12 or 15).
- On the last count/beat children must be back on their starting spot.
- Try again – how far can they travel? What interesting shapes and movements can they make? (If space is a problem, divide class in half, each half to watch the other.)

The hoops (or mats) game

- Teacher puts hoops (or mats) in spaces round the floor.
- At given signal (or when the music starts), children dance anywhere in the room, outside the hoops/mats, not touching each other.

- At signal (or when the music stops), children move into hoops or on to mats as quickly as they can (if space is a problem, divide class in half to watch each other –looking for good dancers).

Statues

- Children move to music or to the rhythm of a drumbeat; when the music stops, children must freeze quite still.
- See if children can hold the frozen shape without moving.
- Tell them what shape you want them to make next time the music stops, eg soft/strong, high/low, tall/small, etc.

Note: many other playground and party games are suitable for warm-up activities.

Movement ideas

The main movement ideas selected for each lesson should be explored and developed in a variety of ways using repetition and contrast. The basic elements of movement include body parts, body moves, body steps and body shapes – all will be needed for exploring movement.

Body parts

Children need help in developing a sense of their whole body, and of the parts that make up this physical whole. One way to develop body awareness is to talk them through various body-sensing experiences, to help them build up a vocabulary of the body and to experience a keener sense of their physical selves. The following are some body-awareness activities:

Body sensing

- Children lie down, quite still, and listen to sounds around them (teacher may add sounds, eg tapping, humming, walking, rustling paper).
- Think about each part of your body that is touching the floor – how does it feel?
- Imagine the shape of your body, think about each part of your body: right foot/left foot, etc.
- Feel yourself breathing: take a deep breath, breathe out very slowly.
- Lying on the floor, lift up one part of the body at a time, let it drop down again.
- Wriggle your fingers; wriggle your toes; wriggle your nose!

It is important for children to discover which parts of the body perform which movements. They need to find out the parts and functions of the body as well as the poetry of its use. There are different ways of categorising the body parts, such as upper/lower or trunk/limbs. Outer/inner part classification is as follows: **Outer parts** include head, neck, shoulders, rib cage, stomach (or tummy), hips, back, arms, elbows, wrists, hands, fingers, legs, knees, ankles, feet, and toes. **Inner parts** include heart (blood), lungs (breath), muscles, bones and joints.

Much of this awareness can be developed in the classroom through project work such as My Body, with child-size figures labelled with body words, body rhymes, body drawings, and body action words. See also Ourselves (p48).

Body moves

There are many ways of categorising body parts and body moves, including stretching and bending, twisting and circling, lifting and falling, swinging, swaying and shaking. It is useful to list those with which you intend to work in your programme plan. The following are examples of basic body moves:

Head

- Hold head high, stretch neck up; how tall can you stand?
- Stand straight, bend head forward, tuck chin in. Can you see your toes?
- Bend head back; can you see the ceiling above you?
- Nod (say yes with your head), and shake head (say no). Fast and slow.
- Move head from side to side, back side to side and forward side to side.
- Move head round and round. Copy teacher's or partner's head moves.
- What parts of your head can you move? Raise eyebrows, wink/ blink, wrinkle nose, smile please (say 'cheese'), open mouth wide, bare your teeth, puff out cheeks (blow), wiggle your ears...

Trunk

- Bend at the waist, touch your toes, crouch low, curl into a ball, roll over.
- Bend at the waist and lean back – what can you see behind you?
- Twist your upper body left and right, keep feet still!
- Hands on hips and swing those hips from side to side!
- Stick out tummies, bottoms or chests.
- Shake all over, fast and slow.

Arms

- Raise your arms and reach up high, reach for the sky!
- Touch your head and shoulders, knees and toes.
- Swing your arms round and round, forwards and backwards, see how fast!
- Reach out wide, move arms up and down by your side, like a bird flying high and low.
- Swim with your arms, on the spot; swim fast, swim slow.

- Shake your arms up, shake them down, shake those arms all over the town!
- Flop forwards with arms swinging, like an ape, and move round the room.

Fingers and hands

- Wriggle your fingers, feel each one moving on its own; let your fingers dance!
- Clap hands loudly, then very softly, clap in the air, clap the floor, have a happy clappy time!
- Rub your hands till they feel warm, and shake them from the wrist (fast/slow, high/low).
- Use your fingertips to do a skipping dance around you on the floor.
- Let your fingers skip around your body and in the air all around you – above, below, in front, behind, side to side, far and near, etc.

Legs

- Put your left/right leg out and shake it all about!
- Lift a leg, kick a leg, kick it high, kick it low, kick it fast, kick it slow.
- Keep your leg straight, how high can you lift it? Left leg? Right leg?
- Lift one leg back and bend forward, arms out wide; can you balance? On each leg?
- Feet apart, knock your knees, bend them wide, move them out and in, flap your legs.
- Wobble your legs, wibble-wobble jelly-legs!
- Lift leg sideways, right and left, one after the other as quick as you can.

Feet and toes

- Stand on tiptoes, right and left.
- Wriggle your toes, wriggle each toe; are they all there?
- Lift your foot; bend your foot up and down, side to side, round and round.
- Touch the floor with your heel then toe, heel/toe, change feet, heel/toe.
- Do a foot dance, a rain dance, a sun dance, a special-day dance.

Body steps

Because we have two feet, we can use them rhythmically and spatially in eight basic steps. These step actions move the body from one place to another:

- Walk: a transfer from one foot to the other on the ground.
- Run: a transfer from one foot to the other off the ground.
- Leap: a running step from one foot to the other.
- Jump: taking off and landing on both feet.
- Hop: taking off and landing on the same foot.
- Skip: a step hop, changing legs, with an uneven beat.

- Gallop: a run with an uneven beat.
- Slide: a walk with an uneven beat, lead foot sliding.

These steps can be organised in sequences, for example: walk, leading to run and leap; jump, leading to hop and skip; gallop, leading to slide. The following are some activities to help explore and develop co-ordination in body steps:

Marching (to music or drum)

- Find a space, march on the spot, lift knees, hold head high.
- March on spot to given rhythm ('left, right', 'one, two'); swing arms in time with legs.
- Walk around marching to music or drumbeats (no one must touch!).
- Walk and swing arms high.
- Walk and lift legs high.

Walking and running

- Walk or run – freeze on given signal (look at the 'statues': are they strong? Do they move?).
- Skip/hop/jog/jump. Encourage children to change direction. Stop on given signal.
- Fast/slow: accelerate or decelerate on given signal.
- High/low: walk or run high or low (near to ground) on given signal.
- Walk or run, then jump (stretch), land, and stop quite still.

Combining steps

- Walk, leading to run.
- Walk, leading to run and leap.
- Walk/run, changing to hopping.
- Jumping, leading to hopping, changing to skipping.
- Children create their own walk/run/jump/hop/skip dance to music or given beat.

Galloping and sliding

- Children gallop, as if they were horses, not touching each other.
- A gallop slowing to a slide (with feet brushing the floor) slowly stopping.
- Children gallop/slide in pairs, holding hands.
- Children gallop/slide in pairs, one after the other (then change leader).
- A group of children gallop/slide in line, weaving patterns of movement.

Body shapes

Every body has a shape, even when it is not moving. We can all create body designs in space: designs that are still (shapes), and designs that move (dancing shapes). The following activities explore and develop awareness of variety in body shape. Make the shape and hold it as still as you can. See what shapes you can make:

Irregular shapes ('crooked man' movements)

- Make 'crooked' fingers: bend fingers (use both joints, both hands); clench/unclench hands.
- Twist the hands, bend wrists backwards and forwards, inwards and outwards. Use sharp, quick movements, hold until given signal, eg on castanets.
- Bend elbows out, up and down; do an elbow dance.
- Move head forwards, sideways, backwards, etc. On given signal, change your head!
- Bend trunk (from the waist), bend knees and ankles, knock your knees, twist your feet.
- Stand still. On given signal stick out one part of your crooked body, eg hip.
- Walk in your crooked shape, stop on signal and change shape!

Regular shapes (tall/small, wide/narrow)

- Start in a small shape (like a seed), slowly rise until body has grown tall and stretched high.
- Move slowly/quickly from tall, to small and narrow.
- Move from small to wide, then to tall and wide (really stretch out!).
- Change your shape and size. At given signal, hold it. Can you make a circular/round shape?
- Walk in your shape and size. Change at given signal. Are you in good shape?
- Divide the class into two and try this dance: tall/wide people move into the centre and make a circle. Small/narrow people move through the tall/wide people's legs, then turn and move out again.

Circles

- Draw circles in the air with one finger, using finger joints.
- Draw circles with all fingers, using wrist joints.
- Draw large circles with whole arm, using shoulder joint.
- Do the above using both hands.
- Put hands together (palms touching) and make large circles in the air.

Drawing shapes

(Initially it is a good idea for the children to copy the gestures of the teacher.)
- Draw a shape in the air with your finger, eg letters, numbers, simple geometrical shapes.
- Draw the shape with the whole hand (moving wrist/elbow joint).
- Draw the shape using the whole arm (moving elbow/shoulder joint).
- Draw the shape using both hands/arms (and by putting both hands together).
- Make a dance with your hands in the air (hands meeting and turning around each other, fingers wriggling or pointing).

Changing shapes

- Sit on the floor. Notice your body is making a shape. Your shape is different from the next person's. On three I want you to sit in another shape. One, two, three. Now find another shape. One, two, three ...
- Make some more strange shapes: a bent shape (bend arms, legs, whole body), a stretched shape (include fingers and toes), a twisted shape, a round shape.
- Make a shape you have never seen before.
- Make a shape standing on one leg.
- Move around in your shape without touching anybody. When you hear the signal, change shape.

Exploring movement

All movement involves space: moving in your own space and moving in the space shared by others. Even when a person is not moving, their body is making a shape in space, at a certain level. When a body moves it has direction, size, place, focus and pathway. All these elements can help to extend and explore any kind of movement. These elements can be summarised as:

- **Shape:** body design in space.
- **Level:** low, medium and high levels of space.
- **Direction:** forwards, backwards, sideways.
- **Size:** big, little.
- **Place:** on the spot, moving through space to another place.
- **Focus:** direction of gaze.
- **Pathway:** straight, curved, circular, zigzag, etc.

Movements can be characterised by different kinds of force. Words used to describe the force of the movement can be first introduced and demonstrated by the teacher. Later, children should be able to use the vocabulary themselves to describe what they have done. Examples of ways of describing force are soft, light, strong, heavy, sharp, jerky, smooth, and sustained. All movements can be altered by changes of force; for instance movements can be sharp or smooth, strong or light; they can be held in tension, or be loose and free-flowing. Movements also vary in time. They have a rhythm, an underlying beat or pulse, that can be decided by the teacher or child. They always have a speed (fast or slow), and a duration (long or short). We need to help children explore contrasts in all these elements, and help them describe what they have done.

Children need to develop the language of dance. One way of describing movement is through imagery. Imagery can be a wonderful stimulus for dance – 'Show me a flower growing', '... a wild horse galloping', '... a branch swaying in the wind'– but it can also be a limiting factor. Children readily get 'in role', and see dance as a form of play. The danger in using imagery is that children focus on trying to be, for example, a prowling cat, rather than on the kind of movement they use to portray a cat. A good way to introduce and to explore movement is through interpreting the imagery present in poems, stories or ideas.

The following offer some possibilities for helping children to explore movement. A stimulus can come from a rhyme, song or image, a poem, story or idea. Children will have their own ideas of what their movements are like. All these ideas can be developed through writing, drawing, topic work or story-telling.

Soft, light movement

Move softly like balloons floating, birds, butterflies, fairies or elves, floating feathers, flickering candles, ghosts, kites, kittens, falling leaves, sailing boats, smoke, drifting snowflakes, the Sandman, summer clouds, Will o' the Wisp ...

Strong, heavy movement

Move in a strong, heavy way, like a person lifting a heavy weight, chopping wood, digging, a bear, a bulldozer, a cart-horse, an elephant (an elephant after a big dinner), a farmer lifting a bale, a giant, a gorilla, a moon-walker, a monster, a rhinoceros, a seal or walrus, a stormy wave, a train, a weightlifter ...

Sharp, jerky movement

Move in a sharp, jerky way, like busy bees, the Crooked Man, frogs, Jack Frost, grasshoppers, lightning, lizards, machines, mechanical toys, puppets, robots, sparklers, woodpeckers ...

Smooth, sustained movement

Move smoothly, like an aeroplane, a bird, a caterpillar, a cat, a fish, cream being poured from a jug, a glider, things growing, ice melting, the moon or sun, skaters, a tightrope walker ...

Movement which grows bigger and collapses

Move like a balloon inflating/deflating, breathing, candle flame rising/snuffed out, flowers unfolding/wilting, the moon waxing/waning, paper screwed up/unfolded, plants growing/dying, tides rising/falling, a bath filling/emptying, shadows growing/shrinking, a snowman growing/melting ...

Moving up and down

Move up and down, like an aeroplane, a seesaw, a bouncing ball, a candle, a falling star, a fireman, things growing, hands (conducting music), Humpty Dumpty, Jack-in-the-box, kites, lifts, rockets, sliding down a slide, snowflakes, the sun, water sucked up/dripping down, umbrellas ...

Moving back and forth, across or around

Move back and forth, like bells ringing, lions in a cage, pistons, sweeping leaves, rowing a boat, a rocking horse, swings, trees in a breeze ...

Move around like curling smoke, a record, a revolving door, a roundabout, a washing machine, a wheel, a windmill ...

Moving high

Move high, like climbing a ladder/mountain, clouds, high-flying birds/eagles, kites, a plane taking off, prancing horses, a rocket launched, a skyscraper, stilt walker, tallest tree ...

Moving low

Move low, like a bird skimming the water, a caterpillar, a creepy crawly, a hunter in the woods, a landing plane, a minibeast, a seal, a snake, a diving turtle, a burrowing worm ...

Moving fast

Move fast, like an arrow, ambulance/fire engine/police car in an emergency, a bullet, a racing car, a cheetah or antelope, a dart, an express train, fireworks, a greyhound, leaves in the wind, a jet plane, a racehorse, rapidly moving water, a speedboat, a sprinter, a squirrel, a shooting star, a swift ...

Moving slow

Move slow, like a baby crawling, a broken-down car, flowers growing, old people, a slow-moving river, slow music, a snowman, a snail, a steamroller, the sun rising/setting, a tortoise, wading in water, walking in mud/thick snow/ in heavy boots/on the moon ...

The key to engaging children at all ages is variety. Try to include the unusual, the interesting challenge. Value the differences in children. They must all work within their capabilities, and the sign of growth is doing something new and something different. All children, even nursery children, can begin in a shape, do some movements that have variety, and end in a different shape. All children can gallop around the room, but with your challenge, they can move down to floor level to make some shapes, and then rise to do some jumps. From moving very lightly they can move very heavily, then freeze and turn – and repeat the routine. By combining actions through repetition and contrast we begin to form a sequence – and a dance is created. Lessons may have the following stages of development:

INTRODUCTION ⟶	MOVEMENT TRAINING ⟶	DANCE THEME
(Presentation and focus on key movements)	(Exploration of movements, building into a sequence)	(Movements linked into a simple dance)

Dance themes

We dance primarily to express what cannot be expressed in words. Dance is a way of communicating through our physical intelligence. We can use the stimulus of words, music or images to help children to become aware of themselves; to become aware of how they can direct their bodies through time and space, and with energy; to help them dance in their own way; and to express themselves in a language which is like no other. Stimulus for dance can come from many sources, such as:

- Words: action words and movement words put in a sequence.
- Rhymes: body chants, nursery rhymes and poems.
- Music: rhythm, music from different times and cultures.
- Stories: folktales and fairy tales.
- Images: pictures, models and artwork.
- Classwork: topic work across the curriculum.
- Children: their own ideas and suggestions.

The following are dance themes and ideas suitable for young children, which can be presented, adapted and developed in many different ways.

Teacher tips
- Introduce free dancing as a challenge about halfway through the term.
- Encourage children to dance as soon as the music starts, not to look at others!
- When the music stops they must hold their shape, ready for the next music.

Free dancing
- Everyone dances at the same time to whatever music is being played.
- The music should be a short sequence.
- When the music stops everyone stops, and listens.
- Play another selection very different from the first; children will enjoy the contrast.
- Encourage variety of expression: 'How many different ways can you dance?'

Ourselves/my body
- Children copy teacher in touching different parts of their body, eg 'Head, shoulders, knees and toes, knees and toes'.
- Explore movement of different body parts : head, trunk, arms, hands and fingers, legs, feet and toes.
- Combine two or more movements, eg walk on tiptoes circling arms, sitting down clap both hands and feet.
- Mirror dance: copy the body movements of the teacher/your partner; hold a 'conversation' together using movements only.
- Sticky dance: alone or with partner find ways of meeting and parting different parts of the body (pretend they are sticky and hard to pull apart!).
- Partner dance: walk behind your teacher/partner and copy hands, head, trunk, legs, feet in different ways.
- Skeleton dance: shake them bones to suitable music, eg negro spiritual *Dem Bones*.

Teacher tips
- Use and encourage children to use body language.
- Create a large body chart with jointed limbs to display and discuss.
- Ask children to draw themselves in a dance pose.

People who help us

The actions of people who help us provide good starting points for movement and dance. Examples of such people include: fire fighter, nurse, delivery person, police officer, lollipop person, driver, refuse collector, window cleaner, farmer, caretaker, secretary, and soldier.

Sample lesson: Fire fighter

Warm up:	Children mime driving a fire engine, moving quickly on signal, not touching each other (use quoits as 'steering wheels', use bell as start/stop signal).
Movement ideas:	a) Arm swinging (hose), heavy movements, high/low, left/right. b) Climbing (ladder), using arms and legs in time, reach high/knees high. c) Stepping (through window, over objects), large, careful steps, balance. d) Tiptoeing (across hot floor), tiptoe, soft, light steps. e) Chopping (burning door, to rescue?), heavy chopping movements, high/low. f) Lifting (rescuing), low, heavy movements.
Dance themes:	**1. Fire fighting** Link into dance sequence on theme of fire fighting: driving, hosing, climbing, stepping, tiptoeing, chopping, lifting – then reverse this sequence. **Resources** (optional): quoits (as driving wheels). **2. Fire dance** Start on floor level. A dance of flickering flames; fingers and toes first, hands and arms, slowly rising, include body/trunk and leg/foot movements; move as the flames spread, end by jumping and leaping. Stop on signal and slowly collapse back onto floor and flicker out. **Resources:** Music (optional): da Falla's *Ritual Fire Dance*, Dukas or Grieg (ref p120). Streamers or shakers of flame-coloured paper or ribbon (hand-held). **3. Caught in the fire** Possible movements include: waking, looking all round, rising from floor level, moving low, pushing through smoke, dropping to floor (for air), moving quickly along floor, rising, and running for safety.

Toys

Using things that move, such as home-made puppets, dolls, toys, etc, can be very stimulating for young children. Such toys can be used in dance to illustrate simple movements; for example, a soft, floppy animal, a ball, a cotton-reel snake, a simple mechanical toy, a spinning top, a plastic or rubber snake, a rocking toy. Ask the children: 'What does it do?' (make it move); ask: 'Can you do that?'. Encourage children to make similar movements; use action words to help them define these movements. Involve different body parts and body shapes: practice these singly, then in simple combinations.

A toyshop dance

Toys come to life at night, when the clock strikes 12! Each child is a toy in place in the shop; clock strikes 12, toys slowly awake, move and dance around the shop. When the clock strikes again, all return to their places and go to sleep again.

A puppet dance

The puppet can be a glove or paper bag puppet character; for example, an animal, a clown, a witch, a magician, a king/queen, a soldier, a pirate, etc. Children can do the movement with the puppet, or the puppet can tell the children what to do. Puppet can involve the children in a story such as weaving spells for the witch/magician, performing tricks for the clown, marching for the soldier.

String puppets can also be a good stimulus: look at how the puppet moves. Move like the puppet, rising up slowly, wobbly steps, arms flopping, jerky movements, collapsing down.

Teacher tip
• Make your own collection of puppets, dolls and novelty toys for movement stimulus; give them names, give them their own stories and make them personal.

Mechanical toy dance

Show and discuss the movement of a mechanical toy, or different moving toys. Children to practice movements and make a mechanical or robot dance: jerky, mechanical movements of all parts of their body, straight limbs, bending arms at elbows, etc.

Snake dance

Show the children a toy snake, eg cotton-reel, plastic, rubber, stuffed stocking. Make movements that stretch and curl. Ask: 'What is it doing? Can you do that?' Movements: curl up tight, stretch out long, move slowly/smoothly along the ground, narrow shapes, bend up in the air, look all around, darting movements. Make snake movements kneeling and standing. Music (optional): Tchaikovsky's *Nutcracker Suite*.

Growing things: plants

Sample lesson: Growth of plants, flowers and trees

Warm up:
Seeds are scattered by the wind and blow hither and thither; seeds lie still and are blown again; wind blows soft, wind blows hard; seeds are carried by water, twisting and turning; at last they rest, curled in the earth, awaiting the sun.

Movement ideas:
a) Sit or lie, uncurl one finger from clenched fist. It rises slowly and smoothly. b) Uncurl two, three, four, five fingers at a time. Repeat with two hands uncurling.
c) Curl up close to the ground; grow slowly, stretching up to the sun.
d) Make a tree shape: wide/narrow/tall/bent, with strong limbs. Change shape.
e) Trees blow and bend in the breeze, leaves (fingers) flutter.
f) Make flower shape: unclench and stretch hands like an opening flower.
g) Become a climbing plant (eg, ivy), spread along the ground, creep up walls, cling, etc.

Dance themes:
1. Growth of chosen plant/flower/tree: link sequence of movements.
2. Half class are flowers (still), half are busy bees moving between flowers.
3. Growth through the seasons: seeds; growing; withering.

Animals

Sample lesson: Growing frogs

Warm up: Running, hopping on one leg and then the other; jumping and then frog-hopping (crouched jumps).

Movement ideas:

a) Frogspawn inside jelly, wobbling ('wibble-wobble'). Lying down, wobble to sound of a tambourine.

b) Grow into tadpoles: lying down, curled, stretch both legs together.

c) Moving tadpoles: along ground, using arms, legs together.

d) Growing into frog: one leg at a time, stand on four legs, frog hop around room.

e) When winter comes frogs hibernate, curled in a warm place.

Dance theme:

1. Combine movements into a frog-growing dance.

2. Use story (eg, *Frog and Toad* by Arnold Lobel) as dance stimulus.

3. Use rhyme or song (eg, *Frog he would a wooing go*) as stimulus.

The seasons

Seasonal events, stories and rituals from different cultures and faiths provide a rich source of ideas for dance. The following are some dance themes relating to different seasons of the year:

Autumn dance
• Leaves falling, flying, fluttering, drifting softly to the ground.
• Leaves blown by the wind, whirl, swirl, twist and twirl.
• Flowers fade and shrivel, droop and drop down; fungi rise and grow.
• Birds fly south, some alone, some in flocks, stopping to rest on branches.
• Squirrels hunt and store nuts, animals curl into small places to hibernate.
• Spiders weave their spiral webs, butterflies have a final flutter-by.
• Gathering in the autumn harvest, picking fruit, digging vegetables, bringing in the corn.

Hallowe'en dance

- The good witch rides on a broomstick, sweeps cobwebs out of the sky, waves her wand to make wishes come true.
- The wicked witch is bent and scary. She stirs a cauldron and weaves magic spells.
- The black cat is proud; it prowls around and is ready to pounce.
- Bats fly by night; they swoop and glide, and in the day they sleep upside down!
- Ghosts float, sway, and drift smoothly along; suddenly they are gone!

(For Hallowe'en poems see *Witch Words* and *Ghosts Galore*, ed Robert Fisher. Published by Faber.)

Teacher tip
- Use percussion accompaniment.

Guy Fawkes – firework dance

- Flames leap up in a dancing fire (see Fire dance p49).
- Rockets shoot up (leap), briefly shower sparks, and sink down (collapse).
- Catherine wheels whirl round (whirl parts of the body).
- Roman candles shower coloured sparks (arms/trunk movements).
- Bangers explode (jump, arms and legs wide).

Winter dance

- Jack Frost comes out at night to paint the trees and grass with frost. He paints frosty pictures on the windows, and pinches our fingers and toes (sharp jerky movements).
- Snowflakes come drifting down; they whirl and twirl in the wind, and fall slowly and quietly to the ground.
- To keep warm we stamp our feet, jump, and run on the spot; we swing and beat our arms.

- We dance in the snow, build snowmen, throw snowballs, and help to shovel snow; it is hard to walk in thick snow.
- The snowman grows until he is big and fat; he does a clumsy dance, and is melted by the sun.
- Ice freezes into a hard shape; icicles hang down; slowly the sharp ice melts.
- We skate over the ice, forwards and back, in patterns, with a partner or in a long line.

Christmas customs

- Santa's reindeer are swift and light; they shake their horns and paw the ground, pulling Santa's sleigh from house to house.
- The Christmas tree is cut down (or dug up) and carried home. It stands tall, with long arms.
- Candles flicker and dance; finally, they sink.
- Bells ring; when you pull the bell rope they swing high and low, and slowly stop.
- Christmas presents may come to life (see Toys p50).
- Other dance themes include The Twelve Days of Christmas, and The Christmas Story.

Spring dance

- March winds blow hard and soft; trees sway, kites fly high, arms of windmills swing round.
- April showers pitter-patter all around, splash on the streets and sink in the ground.
- Birds fly back to mate in pairs, they swoop and glide, and build their nests.
- Animals and insects wake from hibernation and slowly emerge from their winter homes.
- Bulbs grow, buds unfurl and flowers reach towards the sun.
- We dance to greet the spring – like hares and rabbits and spring lambs.

Summer dance

- We play summer games in the open air – we run, hop, skip, jump and climb.
- On swings we move back and forth.
- On a seesaw we move up and down.
- On a slide we climb up and slide down.
- On a roundabout we go round and round.

Animals

Stories and rhymes (see below) can illustrate well the diversity of animal movements. So can music such as Saint Saens' famous *Carnival of the Animals*.

How Creatures Move

The lion walks on padded paws,
The squirrel leaps from limb to limb,
Flies can crawl straight up a wall,
And seals can dive and swim.
The worm he wiggles all around,
The monkey swings by his tail,
And birds may hop upon the ground,
Or spread their wings and sail,
But girls and boys have much more fun,
They leap and dance,
And walk and run.
                            Anon

The Ostrich

Here is the ostrich straight and tall,
Nodding his head above us all.
Here is the hedgehog prickly and small,
Rolling himself into a ball.
Here is the spider scuttling around,
Treading so lightly on the ground.
Here are the birds that fly so high,
Spreading their wings across the sky.
Here are the children fast asleep,
And in the night the owls do peep,
Tuit tuwhoo, tuit tuwhoo.
                            Anon

Teacher tip
• Collect your own anthology of animal poems and rhymes to use as stimulus for dance. Illustrate these with drawings or magazine pictures, and display in the classroom.

The following themes could each be a focus for stories, poems, artwork and dance. One way to begin is to ask 'What does this animal do? How does it move?' Choose action words on which to base a series of movements.

Pets
• Dogs run, jump and chase; when wet, they shake themselves all over; when tired, they stretch out to sleep.
• Cats can creep low and leap high; they dash and pounce. When angry, they hump their backs and hiss. They wash themselves and curl up to sleep.
• Rabbits jump with front and hind legs, wrinkle their faces when they eat and freeze when scared.
• Guinea pigs, hamsters and mice creep and scamper.
• Ponies trot and gallop.

(For poems see the anthology *Pet Poems* ed Robert Fisher. Published by Faber.)

Wild animals

• Lions and tigers prowl with slow heavy steps; they creep when they hunt and raise their heads to roar.
• Monkeys run around with their hands touching the ground, climb and swing through trees, and scratch themselves for fleas!

- Elephants have a long swinging trunk; they plod along slowly and heavily and love to roll in the mud!
- Camels are hump-backed; their heads swing when they walk. They kneel down to rest.
- Kangaroos can run and take big jumps. Ask: 'How many of your jumps equal a kangaroo's jump?'

Farm animals

- Lambs jump and play in the fields; when they see you they stop suddenly and stare.
- Chickens scratch and peck the ground for food, flap their wings, and walk jerkily.
- Ducks waddle, follow each other in line, and swim in the pond.
- Cows graze and wander contentedly. Bulls sometimes paw the ground and then charge!
- Horses trot, gallop and can jump fences; sometimes they rear, or kick their back legs.

Minibeasts

- Spiders are very shy. They climb up walls, and they have many legs and weave spiral webs to catch their food.
- Bees fly from flower to flower to gather honey; their little wings move very fast.
- Ants crawl around busily, carrying heavy loads. They sometimes crawl in long lines.
- Grasshoppers jump from place to place, then stop and sing (rubbing back legs together!).
- Caterpillars and worms hump themselves to crawl along, raise and wave their heads.
- Butterflies and moths move their wings slowly up and down; when they land they close their wings over their heads.

(For poems see the anthology *Minibeasts*, ed Robert Fisher. Published by Faber.)

Animals of the countryside

- Frogs and toads jump with their long back legs.
- Squirrels hunt for nuts, sit up to eat, and scamper up trees.
- Birds hop on the ground and pull up worms. They swoop and glide in the air and build nests.
- Field mice creep, scamper, and hide in small holes.
- Rabbits (see Pets p55), insects and minibeasts (see above).

Amazing monsters (imaginary animals)

- Be a huge and heavy monster, like the 'Oliphaunt' (JR Tolkien): 'Grey as a mouse/Big as a house/Nose like a snake/I make the earth shake ...'.

- Be a quick, light insect, like the 'Triantiwontigongolope' (C J Dennis): 'There's a very funny insect that you do not often spy, it isn't quite a spider, and it isn't quite a fly...'.
- Be a slithery kind of monster, like a 'Slithergadee' (S Silverstein): 'The Slithergadee has crawled out of the sea; He may catch all the others, but he won't catch me ...'.
- Be a funny flying monster, like the 'Zobo Bird' (F A Collymore): 'Do you think we skip?/Do you think we hop?/Do you think we flip?/Do you think we flop ...?'.
- Be your own funny monster, like the wandering 'Dong' (E Lear): 'Slowly it wanders – pauses – creeps – Anon it sparkles, flashes and leaps ...'.
- Be a very frightening creature, like one coming 'Out of the Dark Wood': 'Out of the dark wood/Comes a twisted evil creature ...'.

(These and other monster poems can be found in *Amazing Monsters*, ed Robert Fisher. Published by Faber.)

Other themes

Circus

- The ringmaster is tall and proud, bows all round, and cracks the whip for the act to begin.
- Clowns do funny walks, slip on banana skins, slide and tumble down.
- The tightrope walker balances slowly and carefully across the rope, sometimes jumps or balances on one foot; at the end he bows.
- Jugglers keep their eyes on the things they are juggling; sometimes they kneel or sit while juggling, and pass things behind their backs or between their legs, ending with a big throw.
- Acrobats do clever tricks, like standing on their hands.
- Trapeze artists swing backwards and forwards.
- Sometimes there are performing animals – which could you be?

Transport

- Bicycles: first you mount, then you pedal (sometimes you wobble); can you use arm signals for going right and left?
- Boats: can be sailed (leaning with the wind), or rowed to and fro, or paddled along.
- Cars: move off slowly, drive carefully, keep left, stop at traffic lights (teacher could use red/amber/green card signals); keep both hands on the wheel!
- Trains: stop at stations, sometimes go through tunnels, pull many carriages.
- Planes: take off and zoom high in the sky; they bank their wings when going in a curve. A good pilot makes a smooth landing.

Story-book characters

Many traditional and modern stories can be used as a stimulus for dance, for example:

- *Jack and the Beanstalk*: growing from seed into beanstalk; Jack climbing; giant's steps; Jack escaping; climbing down beanstalk; chopping down beanstalk; beanstalk collapses.
- *Peter Rabbit*: creeping into Mr Mcgregor's garden; hiding; running to escape.
- *The Pied Piper*: playing his flute; dancing through the streets; boy hobbling after.
- *The Hare and the Tortoise*: the fast hare stops and falls asleep, the tortoise plods on to win.
- *Where the Wild Things Are*: wild things having a rumpus–what is a rumpus?

Teacher tip
• If using stories or poems, keep them short; take only part of a well-known story, so that interest is focused on developing movement rather than the narrative of the story. Focus on working with two or three actions, images or feelings.

Teacher tip
• Be prepared to change the story to suit your needs. Allow children the chance to go through the story actions again. Let half the class watch the performance of the other half.

Sample lesson: Rumplestiltskin

Warm up:	Free dancing; freeze when music stops or on drum signal.
Movement ideas:	Walking, leading to running; hopping and skipping on the spot; making body shapes; changing levels.
Dance theme:	Discuss story up to where Rumpelstiltskin (R) is dancing around his fire, singing his name…

a) Fire: sit and show the flames of R's fire.
b) R is a strange little gnome; show his shape. How would he move?
c) R skips around fire; add hopping and a turn or a jump.
d) R dances on the spot, using whole body, singing his song. Continue the story up to the final name-guessing, eg 'Is your name "Bandylegs…?"', etc.
e) R laughs at the wrong names: how does his body laugh?
f) When asked 'Is your name Rumpelstiltskin?' what does R do? (R stamps and stamps, and disappears through the ground!).

Nursery rhymes and songs

Many nursery rhymes and songs are suitable for movement and interpretation through dance, for example:

- The Crooked Man
- Humpty Dumpty
- The Sandman
- Here We Go Round the Mulberry Bush
- Little Miss Muffet
- The Grand Old Duke of York
- One, Two, Buckle My Shoe
- There Was a Princess Long Ago
- Here We Go Looby Loo
- If You're Happy and You Know It
- One Finger, One Thumb Keep Moving.

Teacher tip
- Collect action rhymes and keep them in a book on classroom display. Add words and change popular rhymes to suit your own purposes. Create and memorise your own rhymes.

Raise your hands above your head,
Clap them, one, two, three;
Rest them now upon your hips
Slowly bend your knees.
Up again and stand erect,
Put your right foot out;
Shake your fingers, nod your head,
And twist yourself about!

Slip one and two , (Children slide
two steps to the left)
Jump three and four,
Turn around quickly
And sit on the floor.
Clap one and two,
Nod three and four,
Jump up again,
And be ready for more.

Rhythm dance

In addition to nursery rhymes and songs, a good lead into dance is through clapping and rhythm games, such as the following:

■ Clapping rhymes: teacher claps a rhythm or rhyme; class tries to reproduce it exactly. Children sit in pairs, one claps a rhythm and the other copies it; each pair claps a rhyme and class tries to repeat it; one claps the rhythm, the other moves to the rhythm.

■ Clapping rhythms: 'If you're happy and you know it clap your hands ...' (teacher claps rhythm, children copy); as above but clap other parts of the body, eg heads, shoulders, knees and toes; then move your body while clapping rhythms.

■ Name rhythms: sit in a circle. Each says name three times, then each says name and adds hand/arm movement; then arm/hand movement only. Stand and choose leg movement, then move to the rhythm of your name.

■ Word rhythms: teacher or child repeats chosen words or sounds as before (first sitting/arm movements, then standing/leg movements, then moving round the room).

■ Clapping partners: face partner; clap each other's right hands then left hands four times; clap both hands with your partner four times, clap your own hands four times; partner claps hands while you skip around him/her, then you clap while your partner dances around you. Repeat. (Accompany with a folk dance record. This will be a good introduction to folk dancing.)

Folk dance

Folk dance is a social activity, characteristic of all cultures and is a living tradition, best learnt from a dancer. Find out if there are any folk dance traditions in your area. Do the children or their families already know any folk dances? Invite them to share their knowledge with you and your class. Find out what folk dance experience is available to you in your area and try to give your class at least one folk dance learning experience during the school year (eg, a Maypole dance). For examples of folk dances see *Active PE* Book 2.

There is nothing to stop you from creating your own folk dance. The following are some folk dance skills that can be developed using folk dance music:

• Walking to the music, eg eight steps.
• Children stand on the spot and mark time, eg for eight beats.
• Repeat above holding hands with a partner, first forwards, then backwards.
• Repeat the three stages above with a skipping step.
• Repeat but vary steps – long/small steps and skips. Add hops or jumps.
• Add other body movements, eg nod/shake head, shrug shoulders, shake hands, point toe and tap it (four or eight times), tap heel, tap heel/toe (change feet), clap hands, link arms, etc.
• Try moving in formations, eg circles, or sets of eight partners following a front couple (the front couple make an arch for the others to go through; each pair is given a turn).

Music for dancing

Many of the songs that children learn in school can be used as a stimulus for dance, simply by listening to the rhythm and moving in time. Others will have words which suggest movement, for example: 'Oh we can play on the big bass drum/and this is the way we do it ...' . There is a wealth of music for children to listen and move to, from pop music, TV theme tunes, jazz, folk, classical, to collections of music from many cultures and BBC sound effects. Examples of music that can provide a stimulus for dance, movement or gymnastics are given in the Resources section (pp119–121).

Conclusion

The aim of the concluding activity is to cool down and stretch the children's bodies at the end of the class, and to provide a calm and orderly end to the lesson. It could include slow and gentle actions, and/or a period of complete peace and relaxation.

- Slow-motion activities involve children performing progressively slower and more heavy movements, until they eventually collapse, completely relaxed.
- Flowing motions: on the spot, eg wave arms and body like a tree blown by a dying breeze until only the leaves (fingers) are fluttering.
- Finding a place to rest, eg an animal looking for and finding the ideal resting or sleeping place, collapses, stretches body and completely relaxes.
- 'Dead lions': each child is completely still and relaxed, listening to the teacher or to silence.
- Body-sensing activities (see p40) are appropriate both at the beginning and end of sessions.

Assessment and record keeping

The following is a checklist for assessing and recording the progress of children in dance at Key Stage 1.

The children can:
1 Move in their own space.
2 Stop quite still on a given signal.
3 Follow a simple rhythm, eg by clapping.
4 Follow simple movement directions, eg 'left'/'right'.
5 Follow a partner's movement.
6 Interpret music freely through dance.
7 Skip to music.
8 Distinguish between quick and slow movements.
9 Move in response to different percussion sounds.
10 Create own movement patterns.

For Assessment for dance see pp103, 105.
For Resources for dance see pp119–121.

Games and athletics

'I like games because you don't have to learn anything – you just do it. But if you want to get better at games you have to practice.'

(six year-old)

At the beginning of the infant stage children should be allowed to play freely. Games and athletics fit naturally together at Key Stage 1, and are included here as one combined theme.

Athletics involves experience of running, jumping and throwing activities, concentrating on developing speed and distance in running, height and distance in jumping, and accuracy and distance in throwing. Games involves using a variety of games equipment, including balls and playbats of different sizes, beanbags, hoops, skipping ropes, and, where appropriate, specially designed equipment for children with physical disabilities. Children should experience a variety of ways of sending, receiving and travelling with a ball. They should have opportunities to play and make up games with simple rules as individuals, and later with partners and in small groups. Their experience of games play should include the athletic elements of running, jumping and throwing, as well as awareness of rules, space and of other players.

Effective teaching of games and athletics, as with other areas of PE, will include experimenting, explaining and instructing, questioning and listening to children, observing and assessing their progress, and providing feedback on their progress and achievement. This section provides the following guidance on teaching games and athletics at Key Stage 1:

- What to teach – games and athletics in the National Curriculum.
- Lesson planning.
- Skills development.
- Sports days.

What to teach   games and athletics in the National Curriculum

Competitive games, both individual and team, are an essential part of any programme of physical education. They are part of our national heritage and offer a range of educational opportunities. To explore to the full those opportunities it is necessary to offer pupils a balance of games experiences.'

(PE for ages 5–16, 1991)

The Statements of Attainment in the National Curriculum say that at the end of Key Stage 1, by the age of seven years, pupils should be able to:

- plan and perform safely a range of simple activities and linked movements in response to given tasks and stimuli;
- practise and improve their performance;
- describe what they and others are doing;
- recognise the effects of physical activities on their bodies;
- begin to co-operate with others.

The Programmes of Study say that children should:
- experience running, jumping and throwing activities, concentrating on accuracy, speed, height, length and distance;
- experience using a variety of games equipment including, where appropriate, specially designed equipment for pupils with physical disabilities;
- experience elements of games play that include chasing, dodging, avoiding and awareness of space and other players;
- be given opportunities to make up and play games with simple rules and objectives that involve one person and a limited amount of equipment, extended to working with a partner when ready.

At the beginning of Key Stage 1 children should:

PLAY FREELY

ENJOY MAXIMUM ACTIVITY

PRACTISE LEARNED SKILLS

EXPLORE NEW SKILLS

The units of work planned for Key Stage 1 should aim to cover the Statements of Attainment and Programme of Study, including:
- Games skills: involving ball skills, hoop skills, rope skills, and bat/ball skills which aim to develop hand-eye co-ordination, foot-eye co-ordination and space awareness.
- Athletics skills: involving running, jumping and throwing activities.

These units should include the use of balls of various textures and sizes, beanbags, hoops, ropes, quoits, and a variety of playbats.

Lesson planning

When preparing for a lesson, think about a change of clothes for yourself, as well as for the children: wear trainers outdoors, and suitable warm clothing. Have your games lesson outside whenever possible; be positive about cold or poor weather – all the more reason to be active all the time – provided it is not too wet! Games is an all-year-round curriculum requirement, so try to transfer to an indoor space if there is no outdoor opportunity.

It is helpful to make a list of planned activities, and to carry it, for example, in your watch strap, as a memory aid. It is also helpful to disperse the equipment around the edges of the activity area for ease of access and an organised approach to distribution, before the lesson starts. Remember, walking to the session is part of the lesson. Encourage poise, control, and consideration for others. Look for links in lesson-planning with other areas of study in the class (see Cross-curricular links p17). Lesson plans for games and athletics might take this form:

Warm up
Begin the lesson with vigorous activity, involving stretching, walking, running, jumping, or skipping. These warm-up activities may then be exercised in a game involving the whole class, and the teacher (see below).

Skills development
Children learn to experiment with movement and develop skills through the use of games apparatus, either individually or with a partner.

Small-game activity
Games can be created by the children and/or directed by the teacher and played individually, in pairs, or small groups of three or four children.

Conclusion
This could include either:

- A whole class game – possibly involving the teacher (see overleaf).
- A class-directed, controlled, quiet exercise or sequence of moves.
- An individual skill practised previously.

During the lesson
- Use skills to support the game.
- Use games to reinforce the skills.
- Use brief instructions.
- Use brief demonstrations.
- Allow time for questions.
- Everyone active – no queues.
- Use mixed pairs/small groups.
- Have fun!

For each lesson you may wish to choose one or two activities from each of the following sections: games/warm-up activities to begin the lesson, followed by skills development and small-game activity. These activities are graded in order of difficulty, the first starting with children beginning Key Stage 1, and progressing towards activities appropriate for the end of Key Stage 1.

Games to begin and end

The following are short games which can be used to begin or end a lesson. These may be adapted or developed to suit your class or teaching purpose. The children may well have games of their own to suggest, or may suggest variations on the ones listed. Try to link the chosen game with the warm up or skills development activities.

What's the time Mr Wolf?

Class walk behind the teacher (who is the wolf); when wolf turns, all stop and chant 'What's the time Mr Wolf?' Wolf chants a time, and turns to continue walking. When wolf calls 'Dinner time!' children run away to safe area, and wolf tries to catch them. A caught or chosen child may become the wolf.

Statues

A shape to make such as an elephant, a goldfish, a tree, etc. Children freeze in that shape. Teacher chooses children to demonstrate the funniest/most still/most realistic shape.

Numbers

Children walk, jog, or skip in any direction, without touching each other. Teacher signals children to stop by calling out a number for children to make by joining hands in a group circle. The number 3 means three children must join hands in a group. Variations include making simple sums such as 2+2, 3+1, etc or numbers called in another language.

Shapes

Children walk, jog, or skip in any direction, without touching each other. Teacher signals children to stop by calling out a geometric shape to make with part of their body; for example: 'Triangle – with your arms.'

Freeze!

Children move like frogs/snakes/soldiers/giants, etc. When teacher calls 'Freeze!' all stop still. Any movement is lightly observed, and no dropping out is necessary.

Simon says

Children obey teacher's command to make an action eg 'Touch your nose', but must copy the action only if it is prefixed by 'Simon says'. Children may have 'lives' which are lost if they make a false move (or no action when they should have moved) rather than having to drop out.

Grandma's footsteps

Teacher (grandma) stands in a hoop; the children creep towards her. Teacher turns suddenly to catch (by spotting a child moving) any mover, who then must return to the starting place. The aim is to be the first to reach grandma's hoop.

Tom Tiddler

Teacher is the catcher or Tom Tiddler (the optional/traditional name). On a signal, children run across a given area and try not to be caught (touched) by the teacher/Tiddler. If touched the child helps the teacher to catch others when they next run across. The last two or three to be caught become the new Tom Tiddlers.

Stuck in the mud

Two or three chasers try to tag as many as possible in a set time. If touched, a child stands still with legs wide apart. They can be released by touch, or at a later stage, by someone crawling between their legs. No tagging is allowed if a child is under the legs of a child being released.

Tag

Tail tag: each child tucks a braid in their shorts and on signal tries to collect the tails of others.

Pair tag: when the chaser tags a child they join hands to become a pair; when four are tagged they become two pairs, and so on until all children are caught.

Chain tag: the same as pair tag except groups hold hands in chains five to six children long.

Basket full

Teacher scatters beanbags; as the children try to fill the basket by collecting the beanbags, the teacher empties the basket. Nobody must carry more than one beanbag at a time. The teacher should win sometimes!

Circle bag run

Approximately six children form a circle and are numbered one to six. In turn, children run with a bag around the circle and hand it to number two, and so on until all have had a turn.

Treasure hunt

Teacher calls a signal; the children run to the appropriate corner (if North, South, East or West is called), make the shapes and actions as required, eg digging, climbing, crawling, stretching, reaching, to find the 'treasure'.

Pairs

Children run, skip or jump, without touching. On a signal, pairs of children either link arms, hold hands, stand back to back, or make a pair bridge. There are no losers; anyone left over joins the teacher.

Circle trap

Half the class hold hands high in a circle (the trappers) forming arches; the remainder run in and out of the arches. On the call of 'trap' those caught inside the circle join the trappers, ready for the next round.

Pass the parcels

The class forms a large circle and between two and eight beanbags (the parcels) are given out (evenly spread between the children in the circle). On a signal, children pass the parcels as quickly as they can in a given direction (right or left). Nobody must be caught with two beanbags. The bags must be passed not thrown!

Follow the leader (in small groups)

The actions of the leader must be copied as the children follow in line. At first the teacher calls the actions; later, children can take the role of leaders of their group.

Shadow steps (to be played on a sunny day)

One child runs and swerves, their partner tries to step on the shadow of their head, arm or body. On a signal they change roles.

Jump the streams

The class – or half the class – jump over as many 'streams' (lines marked, or ropes laid out, on the ground) as possible in a set time.

Warm-up activities

The following are some suggested warm-up activities to start the lesson:

- Action songs/rhymes/games to help children acclimatise to the new setting (see pp39–40).

- **Walking, jogging or running in different directions.**
- Fast/slow, change on command.
- Big/little steps, change on signal or in own time.

- Change direction on a given signal.
- Along/over lines in the play area.
- Walk/move like a... (soldier/old person/giant, etc).
- Forwards/backwards/sideways ... look all around as you move – no touching!

- **Running to use all the space in the play area.**
- In different directions and back to starting place on signal.
- As above and then hop/skip/run on the spot.
- Stop on signal to crouch jump (repeat as often as necessary).
- On signal, crouch to touch the ground and then continue running (a).

(a)

  - As above, in a low position/in a high position.
  - Swerve and change direction.
  - Stop on signal/in own time (coach low hips, bent knees).
  - As above and run off in a new direction.

- **Jumping.**
- Small jumps/big jumps.
- Feet together/feet apart.
- With a stretch with one or both arms raised high.
- Forwards/backwards/sideways.
- Over/in/out of hoops, markings, ropes (b).

(b)

  - Crouch, to high stretch, and repeat.
  - Hopping on one or both feet.
  - With two or three steps and jump long/high.

- **Stretching.**
- Free stretching movements to reach high/wide.
- Action games that involve bending/stretching activity, eg I'm a little teapot, Incy wincy spider, Head, shoulders knees and toes.
- Various body parts: head/shoulders/legs/wiggle bottoms/feet.
- Arms swinging/circling/reaching/pressing back/shaking.
- Trunk turning/twisting/bending/arching.

Skills development

The following activities involve individuals or pairs in skills development and games using small apparatus. These can be undertaken as whole-class activities (involving individuals, groups or pairs), or with groups of children taking turns using different kinds of apparatus (see Grids and groups p73).

Beanbags

• Balance a bag on any part of your body: knee, head, shoulder, top of foot (c).
• Balance a bag on the palm/back

(c)

of either hand/head, and walk or move slowly (d).

(d)

• Balance a bag on another part of the body; move in different directions.
• Grip a bag between your knees/ankles/hand and knee, or other part of the body.
• Grip a bag as above and move in different directions.
• Run in different directions with a bag in one or both hands.
• Run in different directions with a bag as above but place bag on the ground and pick up on return (bend your knees).
• Create a sequence of two or three movements with a beanbag, using the skills learnt.
• Toss a bag into a space away from other people; run to pick it up.
• Toss a bag into a hoop lying on the ground, or from one hoop to another.
• Pass a bag to a partner in sitting or standing position (e).
• Throw underarm to a partner in sitting or standing position.
• Pass or throw a bag to a partner in different ways (overhead, between the legs, etc).
• Grip a bag with a partner using different body parts; stationary at first and then moving.

(e)

Large or medium balls

Many of the beanbag activities above can be used as ball activities! Here are some more activities using large or medium playballs which will help develop hand-eye skills and co-ordination:

Handling the ball

These early ball skills are designed to give confidence in handling the ball, and involve touching, holding and running with the ball.

• Hold, touch, and balance the ball with or on different parts of your body.
• Pick up and hold a ball in both hands; stretch high/low/back/forward holding the ball.
• Hand the ball to a partner in front/behind/sideways, etc.
• Sit/lie down or stand and roll the ball over or along different parts of your body.
• Sit/lie down or stand and roll the ball along the floor, in, out and around your body.

(f)

- Run with the ball under one arm (f).
- Skip/hop/jump with the ball in both hands or under one arm.
- Run with the ball, in and out of cones/hoops/beanbags placed randomly in the play area.
- Run with the ball, in and out of cones/hoops/beanbags, with cones, etc placed in a line.

Throwing and rolling

After confidence is gained in handling the ball, throwing and rolling skills can be developed using the following activities:

- Throw the ball underarm with one or two hands; on given signal, run to collect.
- Throw the ball underarm with one or two hands, against a wall. Collect in your own time.
- Roll the ball into a space, watch where it goes and collect on signal.
- Roll and guide the ball all over the play area/in a small space/ forwards/ backwards/sideways.
- Roll and guide the ball around cones/hoops/beanbags spaced randomly in the play area.
- Roll the ball to aim at a target, eg hoop, skittle, marking, or through the legs of your partner.
- Roll the ball, run alongside and pick it up on the move.
- Roll the ball; find different ways to stop it using hands/feet/other (g).

(g)

Bouncing

The following are some activities to develop skills and control in bouncing a play ball:

- Drop the ball from different heights to bounce and catch (hug the ball to your chest).
- Toss the ball progressively higher, and catch it after one, two or three bounces.
- Toss the ball around you, overhead or sideways; let it bounce and then catch it.
- Toss the ball as above, let it bounce and catch it while on the move.
- Bounce the ball on the floor and catch it, either while you are stationary or on the move.
- Bounce and catch the ball around your body in different ways.

(h)

- Pat bounce the ball as many times as possible (h).
- Bounce ball in, out and around a hoop and catch it. How many ways can you do it?
- Bounce the ball into a hoop for your partner to catch (keep your fingers behind the ball as you push it from your chest).

Catching (vary playball size according to need)

Demonstrate and encourage children to practise these catching techniques:

- Keep hands and elbows close together (ready to clasp the ball).
    - Keep palms up (ready to catch the ball) (i).
    - Keep little fingers crossed (to stop the ball slipping through).
    - Keep watching the ball as it goes into your hands.
    - Reach out and hug the ball into your body.

(i)

Most of the beanbag and ball holding, rolling and bouncing activities will have included early catching experience. Catching skills can be further developed by these bouncing and catching activities, which are listed in order of difficulty:

(j)

- Toss the ball against a wall to bounce and catch it, then throw and catch it with no bounces (j).
- Toss the ball a few centimetres into the air, and catch it.
- Gradually toss the ball higher; encourage the child to move under the ball to catch it.
- Sitting opposite a partner, roll, toss or bounce the ball for your partner to catch.
- Opposite a partner, roll, bounce or throw the ball, crouching, then standing (k).
- Experiment with different ways of throwing and catching the ball, eg overhead, between the legs, clapping then catching, etc.

(k)

Challenge and competition can be added as appropriate depending on the success of skills practised, or by seeing if they can be accomplished in a given time. Personal challenges may be more appropriate than encouraging children to compete against each other; allow them to demonstrate their successes. To add further variety, these progressive skills can be practised with a partner, or in the games below. For these games the children should be in teams of two to four to ensure maximum activity.

Hand ball games (in teams)

- Children pass the ball from one to the other, from the front to the back child, who then runs to the front to repeat the sequence of passes.
- The game can be varied by passing the ball overhead, under legs or sideways (l).

(l)

• The team can stand side by side to pass the ball; the last child moves to the opposite end of the line on receiving the ball (m).

(m)

• The team standing in line, children roll the ball between their legs (n).

(n)

• Children pass the ball over heads and under legs, alternately, down the line.

Encourage and help children to create their own ball-passing games, as variations on the above. Other ball-passing games include **passing a ball on the move**, with a partner, over the entire playing area. When children are confident, add the challenge of one child trying to **intercept the ball** as it is passed between partners. Remind the players that there is to be no touching each other! On a given signal, change the roles, so that each child has a turn as an interceptor of the ball.

Grids and groups
Many of these ball skills can be practised individually, in pairs, and in small groups. Towards the end of Key Stage 1, children can practise small-group activities in grids or stations.

Group activities in grids or stations
The following is an example of the way children in groups of four can rotate round a course of eight activities organised in grids or areas of the available play space:

Beanbags	Beanbags	Ball	Ball and hoop
(individual skills	(pair/challenge tasks)	(individual skills)	(pair activity)
Ball footskills	Ball footskills	Ball game	Ball
(pair game)	(individual)	(challenge activity)	(passing and catching)

Further challenge and skills development can be introduced as the children grow more confident and competent, for example:

- Introducing and noting personal best scores.
- Achieving a best score within a set time limit.
- Achieving a best consecutive score over a number of turns.
- Achieving a best score with a partner.
- 1 v 1, 2 v 1, 3 v 1 games introduce an element of mild competition.
- Co-operative games in teams of three or four to achieve a team score.

Footskills using large or medium balls

The following activities are aimed at developing a progressive range of footskills, and require that each child has a medium-sized playball.

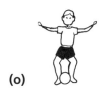
(o)

- Experiment by touching the ball with instep, sole, heel and toes.
- Move the ball forward, walking; keep it close to you and try to avoid everyone else!
- Wedge the ball between your knees/ankles/feet and move in different ways (o).
- Practise jumping over the ball when it is stationary and when it is moving.
- Move the ball in different directions; on a signal, stop it with the sole of the foot.
- Move the ball in different directions around and in and out of hoops, beanbags, or cones placed randomly or in a line.
- Dribble the ball between the legs of half the class who stand in a space with legs wide apart.
- Roll the ball with the sole of the foot, forwards, backwards and sideways; stop on a given signal.
- With children in lines, back to back, or well spaced in the play area, kick the ball with the instep (best) or top of the foot; chase and collect the ball.

(p)

- Kick the ball, chase after it and stop the ball with your foot in different ways (p). (Teach the technique of bending the knee and following through with the leg as you kick. Use the favourite foot first, then try with the other foot.)
- As above, but start with a walk or run-up.
- Kick the ball against a wall, from a stationary position, and then with a walk or run-up.
- Dribble the ball; on a given signal, kick the ball. Collect and repeat.
- Kick the ball at wall markings or between cones, etc, aiming for accuracy.
- Kick the ball as far as you can (**outside**); measure distance with set markers.

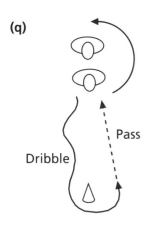

(q)

Pass

Dribble

- One ball per pair. One partner dribbles the ball to a marker or line, and back. Change roles.
- Dribble the ball around a cone, kick it back to partner who repeats. Use each foot alternately to control the ball (q).
- Pass the ball back and forth, using the instep or side of foot; watch the ball; keep the non-kicking foot near the ball.
- As above, but use your worst foot.
- Facing a partner, two to three metres apart. Dribble round your partner and back, pass ball to partner. Change roles.
- Pass the ball to a partner who traps it with their instep and passes back.
- Pass the ball to a partner on the move, all over play area, keep two or three metres apart.
- Shield the ball with your body whilst dribbling in a small area; partner runs behind; change on signal.
- Dribbling in a small area, as above, but partner attempts to touch and steal ball with a foot from front and side. No touching or body contact is allowed.

An element of mild competition can be introduced, eg 'How many can you do in one minute?' ' Can you beat your best score?' and avoids the problem of deciding who is first, second or last.

Small games using foot skills
- **Circle dribbles**: make circles of 12 children, with a ball each. Number the children one, two or three. Call a number, and those children dribble round the outside of the circle back to their place. Variations on this theme include: dribble in and out of children in the circle (r); change direction on a given signal.

(r)

- **Dribble relays**: not more than four per team, in line behind each other: a) each person in turn dribbles around the team and back to their place; b) each person in turn dribbles in and out of the players of the team, who are well spaced; c) (in teams of four to six) each person in turn dribbles and passes with a partner, to a marker and back, then next pair repeats the process.
- **Shooting game**: with a partner. Shoot ball through several small goals spaced around the edge of the playing area. Shoot at a different goal each time. Make four passes between each goal attempt.
- **Tackling game**: in twos or threes. One player dribbles the ball and shields it from two others who tackle, with no body contact, from the front. Only one challenge allowed on each child. Change when possession is lost or on given signal. A variation of this is for children to score through small goals spaced all around the perimeter of the playing area. The number of children intercepting can be altered according to the ability of the children (s).

(s)

- Cones (small goals) 2m apart.
- Ball always in play.
- Score from either side.
- Move to new goal after each attempt to score.

Hoop activities

Generally, large hoops are easier to move into, although smaller hoops can be handled and moved more readily; ensure that two or three sizes are available, to cater for different ages and stages.

There are many activities that may form part of the gymnastics lesson, but can also be used as introductory games activities:

Movement with a static hoop

(t)
- Find different ways to move around/over/in and out of the hoop (t).
- Walk/jump/hop/skip between all the hoops in the activity area.
- Jump in and out of all the hoops (there must never be more than one person in a hoop); find different ways to jump in and out of your hoop.

(u)
- Can you slide under and into the hoop, or roll into and out of the hoop? (u).
- Use hands and feet to move in and out of the hoop.
- Run and jump into the middle of the hoop. Land on two feet.
- Step/jump in/out of a hoop held close to the ground, horizontally, by a partner. Find other ways to cross the rim without touching it.
- Step/jump through a hoop held vertically/diagonally.

Moving the hoop

(v)
- Show ways to move the hoop around/over you. No throwing in the air! (v).
- Hold hoop vertically, on ground, by toes; step through, swing hoop forward over head and back to the ground.
- As above, backwards; how many can you do?
- Speed up until you are skipping. (Repeat process, jumping, instead of stepping.)
- Skip the hoop on the spot/around the play area.
- Spin/twist the hoop around different body parts: waist, ankle, arm, etc.

Rolling the hoop (small/medium hoops are easier)

(w)
- Roll the hoop in different ways along the ground. Stay close to it. (w).
- Use two hands: one on top to guide hoop, one behind to push and rotate.
- Roll hoop between partners, three or four metres apart.
- Can you spin/roll the hoop backwards?
- Spin the hoop, like a top, on the ground.
- While it is spinning can you clap hands/run round it, etc?
- Roll the hoop while walking/jogging/skipping. Stop on signal.

(x)

Games with hoops

- **Horses**: in pairs, holding inside and outside hoop. Horse and rider run freely/run to touch set targets. Change on signal (x).

- **Prisoners**: two or three inside a hoop. Move together in one direction/run to reach set targets/move over and under obstacles (y).

(y)

(z)

- **Hoop relays**: one hoop between four. Include rolling while running/hopping/skipping. Relays can be there and back, or shuttle relays with two children opposite each other, 10–12 m apart. Hoop relays can include passing the hoop/skipping/running through the hoop/rolling the hoop.
- **Musical hoops**: when music stops, or on signal, run inside hoops. Teacher to call number of children. Hoops should be dispersed evenly about the area.
- **Frogs**: in twos and threes with two hoops. A places the second hoop to enable B to jump/step from hoop to hoop in the area (z).
- Ask children to invent their **own games** using one or two hoops, in pairs or small teams.

Rope activities

Children will benefit more from rope activities if they have already experienced the hoop activities. As with the hoops, many of the rope activities that follow include elements of gymnastics, games and athletic skills.

Activities with a rope on the floor

The following activities require the use of one skipping rope per child, laid on the floor:

- Move along or over a rope laid straight along the floor; find a variety of ways to do this.
- Hop, jump, or walk along a rope forwards/backwards/sideways.
- Use hands and feet to travel along or over the rope; make a zig-zag path.

(aa)

- Make a closed or open shape with the rope, or a shape suggested by the teacher to link in with classwork to move in/out/around rope using feet/hands and feet (aa); jump in/out/over shape; make a pattern of steps or jumps in and around the rope.
- Jump with two feet from the rope to land on two feet, be still; jump from outside back inside the rope shape.

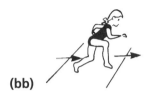

(bb)

- Try the above activities using a one-foot take-off, and a few walking steps and a one-foot take-off.
- Two ropes can be used for the above activity (bb).
- In threes. One to jump over a low rope, loosely held by two others; try a two-footed jump, progress to a one-footed jump.
- A variety of shape and balance activities can also be explored using a rope. See Gymnastics pp28, 30.

Skipping

Skipping has long been regarded as a useful fitness activity in sport. It involves a number of co-ordination skills, and may take some time for young children to master. Children can be encouraged to practice at playtimes if ropes are provided for this purpose.

First, demonstrate to the children the technique of skipping: hold the rope with the arms fairly wide so that it drops behind the ankles; swing the rope forwards over your head to the floor, step over the rope, and stop.

- Invite the children to try to skip on the spot (some will be successful).
- How many times can the children step over the rope while skipping?
- Swing the rope faster; can you step or jump over two, three, or four times without stopping?
- Double-foot jump over rope. Use the same progression as above, but add a small bounce jump between big jumps.

Once the children are skipping, encourage them to:

(cc)

- Create different ways of skipping on the spot or on the move.
- Skip with the rope swinging backwards or sideways.
- Skip and turn on the spot.
- Skip forwards, running, jumping and hopping.

Skipping games and activities

The following are some activities to help develop skipping skills:

- In pairs, one rope each. Match your partner's skipping movements.
- In pairs, with one rope. Skip together (cc).
- In threes and fours with long rope. One or two skip while two turn the rope (dd).

(dd)

- Create your own series of rope activities, for example: skip 20 m, then jump 10 m from rope shape to rope shape, jump six times in a zig-zag along a straight rope and skip backwards ten times on the spot.

Note: races and relays with skipping ropes are not usually a good idea, as they create too much pressure on children and can lead to accidents.

Small-ball activities

Small-ball activities should include experience with soft balls. In developing throwing, catching and striking skills with small balls it is best to use tennis balls. Alternatives are soft rubber and foam balls, which can be slippery to handle, but which are lighter, and are especially useful for indoor play, where damage may be caused by the use of tennis balls.

Throwing and catching skills

Many of the beanbag and large-ball activities can be repeated with small balls (see pp70–73), especially those involving balancing, running, moving, throwing, rolling, bouncing, and catching. The following activities with small balls can be added to those above – remember to allow children to experiment before directing or coaching them.

(ee)

- Balance the ball on front or back of the hand.
- Balance the ball on front or back of the hand, high/low/sideways, using best and worst hand.
- Balance the ball as above, while walking, running, kneeling, sitting, crouching, or lying (ee).
- Run, holding a ball in either hand, to and from a target.
- Holding a ball in either hand, run in and out of cones.
- Roll the ball forwards, run, then stop to pick up the ball and run back to your place.
- Roll the ball in a small area; pick it up on a given signal.
- Bounce the ball with one hand, catch it with two; try low and high bounces.
- Bounce the ball and catch it with left or right hand. Count how many times you are successful!
- Pat bounce the ball with either hand, using a flat palm.
- Catch and bounce or pat bounce the ball: in different directions/in front/behind/left/right; under your legs; changing hands; while turning/lying/sitting/crouching/walking/running to and from target, or in and out of obstacles.

Pair activities (see also beanbag and large-ball pair activities)

- Roll the ball to a partner in various positions (as above), who catches and returns.
- With a partner. Bounce ball with an overarm throw into a hoop placed between you (ff).

(ff)

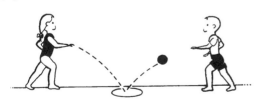

- Throw underarm to a partner, who catches the ball (throw to tummy, cup hands ready to catch, and hug the ball to your body). Begin one metre apart; move further apart when catching is successful.
- Throw underarm to a partner, using one hand to catch.
- With a partner. A rolls ball, B picks it up and throws it back underarm for A to catch.

• Practise underarm throwing and catching: high/low, left/right, in front/behind; move quickly to catch the ball. Encourage catchers to move the feet fast to a good position. Start one to two metres apart for throwing and catching; this distance can be increased or decreased with each success or failure.

• Practise overarm throwing with two lines of children approximately 20 metres apart: each child throws a ball overarm to their partner. All throw when the teacher signals. Encourage the thrower to stand sideways on, with feet well apart, the ball in their fingers, their arm slightly bent above the head, and to chuck the ball towards their partner. To throw the ball at 45º (an ideal angle of throw) is very difficult at this stage.

Dodge ball games

• **Dodge ball**: choose two to six children and give a ball to each one. Their aim is to roll the balls to touch any other child in the class below the knees. Play the game in a restricted area. Count the number of hits rather than withdraw children who are hit (who then become inactive from the game).

• **Circle dodge ball**: is played as Dodge ball, with the throwers outside a drawn circle and the dodgers inside the circle. Once children know how to play, you could organise two or three circle games of ten in a circle, (gg) rather than one big game involving the whole class (five a side).

• **Circle run**: is played with marked small circles as above; the children are numbered one to ten. The teacher calls two, three or four numbers at once for children to run with the ball; run while bouncing and catching, or pat-bouncing the ball around the circle, and back to their place. Which two, three or four can finish first? Variety can be added by changing the direction in which children run.

Ball relays

Relays of all kinds can be organised with only three or four children to a team. One of the best is:

• **Corner spry**: one child stands on a mark one metre in front of the rest of the team, who stand on a line ready to catch the ball in turn. Thrower passes the ball underarm to each team member (who throw it back). On catching the ball, the last child in line runs with the ball to the throwing spot, thrower returns to the team line, and the process is repeated until each child has had a turn as thrower. All line up at the end. Various corner spry games can be created, incorporating the children's ideas. Variations include underarm, overarm, rolling or throwing with one bounce, to each member of the team. The fastest team need not always win. Sometimes look for the quietest team, the neatest throwers/catchers, or the team which does not drop the ball (this may take some time!).

(gg)

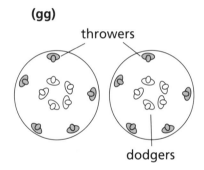

throwers

dodgers

'A' throws   'B' ready to catch

(hh)

• **Wall ball**: play against a wall, with teams of two to four. A throws the ball against the wall for B to catch on the rebound; B then throws for C, who throws for D. Wall ball can be played with rebound and catch, with or without a bounce (hh).

Hitting and striking skills

Foam and air flow balls (approximately 10 cm in diameter) are easier to hit than smaller tennis balls, and will bring more success in the early stages. Each child should be provided with a playbat and ball. Safety considerations should be emphasised, for example: 'Always find a clear space away from others before using a bat'. The following activities will help develop hitting or striking skills.

Using the palm of your hand

• Balance the ball on one hand, holding your arm out in front: high, low, left, right.
• Balance the ball on the other hand.
• Balance the ball, as above on the back of your hand.
• Pat the ball up a few cm, then try patting it higher. Try it with the other hand.
• Pat-bounce the ball on the ground high, low, left, right (ii).
• Pat the ball forward against a wall and then retrieve it.

(ii)

Using a playbat

• Practise holding, gripping and swinging a light, flat bat, to hit an imaginary ball.
• Imaginary hitting, as before, hitting high and low, left and right.
• Practise the previous actions, turning the wrist and hitting with the back of the bat.
• Practise running forwards, backwards, and sideways with a bat in your hand.
• With a bat, pat the ball up a few cm, let it bounce and stop or catch it.
• With a bat, try to hit the ball continuously two, three, four or five times.
• Hit the ball up head high, and try to repeat continuous hits.
• Hit the ball to rebound against a wall with a bounce (jj).
  These activities can all be practised forehand and backhand, and with either hand.

(jj)

Pair activities

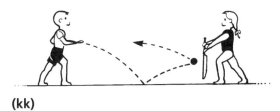

(kk)

• Practise different ways to hit a ball from the hand for a partner to catch (encourage the use of the front and the back of the bat).
• Partner bounces the ball to the striker who hits it back for a catch. Try forehand and backhand. Work together to make an easy catch. Change round after counting ten attempts (kk).

• Play **Wall ball**, hitting alternately at rebounds and allowing one, two or three bounces. How many rebound hits can be achieved continuously by each pair?
• Hit softly to each other, four to five metres apart, with or without a bounce.
• Hit softly to each other, as above, but hit over a line or skipping rope laid flat on the ground.
• Using a playbat or light cricket bat. A, with back to wall, hits bouncing ball back for partner to catch.
• Using a playbat or light cricket bat. As above, with A defending a cone or wall marking.
• Invent your own game using a bat, ball and rope. Let children choose which type of bat and ball to use.
• Using short-handled wooden bats, hit an airflow ball or shuttlecock to each other. Hit up; how many times can you do it? Try using forehand and backhand.

In these activities, co-operative play is of the essence, with children hitting the ball to each other and helping each other. Encourage pairs to display their developing skills to the class.

Games
• **Tennis**: in groups of two or four for continuous tennis. Hit over a rope or bench, and allow for any number of bounces between hits!
• **French cricket**: in groups of three or four. Underarm bowling to hit the batter below the knee; bowl from where ball stopped. Batter may turn to face the bowler; change after six strikes, unless out (leg hit below the knee by the ball).
• **Mini cricket**: in groups of four. Six balls are bowled and struck by each child in turn, then all change round. All start with five runs and add any more scored. If bowled, caught or run out, lose two runs. (Striker can run to bowlers cone or separate cone (ll).)

(ll)

Mini Cricket

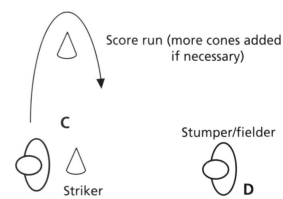

Fielder **B**

Bowler
A

Score run (more cones added if necessary)

C

Striker

Stumper/fielder
D

Children change round A → B → C → D → A → etc

• **Mini rounders**: in groups of four. As above, with batter having three strikes with a small, flat rounders bat. Score by running around one, two or three beanbags or cones; all change round after the batter runs and scores, or is out.

Sample lesson plan

games/athletics for Key Stage 1

Fig 8: Chart of six lessons in games/athletics for Key Stage 1

The chart below offers six sample lessons in games/athletics on the theme of hand-eye co-ordination using beanbags and large balls.

	1	2	3	4	5	6
WARM UP (vigorous exercise)	**Walking** a) Fast/slow, diff directions.Change on signal - big/ small steps. b) **Stretching** whole body high/low.	**Walking/jogging** a) Change direction (i) on signal (ii) in own time. b) Over/along markings on floor. c) Stretching low/ wide.	**Walking/jogging** a) Forward, backwards, sideways. b) Walk like a ... soldier, gymnast, spaceman, giant. c) Curling/stretching all body.	**Walking/jogging/ running** a) Repeat **3 a, b.** b) Stretching to star, tree, leaf shapes. c) Stretching/ twisting like fire-works.	**Running/jumping** a) Different speeds. Stop on signal in space. b) Running and jumping into a space. Be still on landing.	**Running/skipping/ jumping** a) Different speed/direction. b) Rpt **5 b.** Land both feet together.
SKILL DEVELOPMENT	c) **Beanbags** Balance on any body part. Balance on head, shoulder, knee. d) Balance bag on palm/back of hand. Walk slowly. e) Balance bag on any part. Move in diff directions. f) Pass bag around/under/ over body. No dropping!	d) **Beanbags** Repeat any of **1 c, d, e, f.** e) Balance bag on any part. Move slowly on hands and feet. f) Run in different directions, bag in one/two hands. g) Practise stopping and changing direction OFTEN.	d) **Beanbags** Repeat **2 e,f.** e) Balance bag on head, sit, slowly, stand and repeat with arms folded/ other ways? f) Toss bag a few cm high; clap hands to catch. g) As **f** but toss to head high (count number of catches).	**Beanbags or balls** (6 inch diam) d) Repeat **3 f,g.** e) Facing/ sideways with partner, pass bag/ball back and forwards. f) As **e** sitting. g) Throw bag/ ball gently to partner.	**Large balls** (6 inch diam) c) Touch ball with different body parts. d) Roll ball off different parts. e) Throw and catch a few cm high. f) Roll ball in/ around/outside legs with one/two hands.	**Large balls** c) Repeat **5 e f.** d) Teach throw/ catch. e) Find new ways to rebound and catch. f) Roll/bounce ball over whole area. Try different ways. Stop, throw and catch (rpt).
INDIVIDUAL/ PAIR/ GROUP ACTIVITY	g) In pairs (close) hand bag to partner, one/two hands. h) Drop bag into partner's hands. How many?	h) In pairs. Repeat **g, h.** i) Pass beanbag sitting/standing. j) Toss beanbag sitting/standing.	h) Pairs (2m. apart?).Toss bag to partner. Count the catches. i) Balance bag on head, drop to floor, pick up, run round partner twice and change.	h) Pairs. Find ways to grip beanbag between two body parts (eg one hand each, hand/knee, head/head, etc).	g) Pairs. Rpt **4 h.** h) Move with bag gripped between two body parts.	g) Throw and catch in pairs (increase distance with each catch, decrease if dropped).
GAME/END ACTIVITY	i) Make up your own bean bag activity. j) 'Simon Says'. k) Little Peter Rabbit (reception).	k) Class in two halves - A, B. Group A run/crawl through legs of Group B with beanbag in one or two hands.	j) **Beanbag gather** Teacher scatters 30 beanbags. Children gather and place (one at a time) into four baskets while teacher counts or says rhyme, etc. k) What's the Time, Mr Wolf?	i) **Beanbag scatter** Teacher (or team) keeps emptying two or four baskets. Class keep filling (one bag at a time) Is it ever empty/ full?	i) Beanbags balanced on heads/back of hands. Move carefully in/out of half the class who balance bag on another part. j) Granddad's footsteps (reception).	h) Make up a game in pairs, where ball is rolled, bounced and caught. i) Roll ball between legs of half of class, who stand legs apart in spaces. j) Granddad's footsteps (reception).

Sports days

Sports days can be great fun if they are well organised, and provide opportunities for all to succeed at their level. They can also help meet many of the aims of the National Curriculum through activities involving planning, preparation and performing, for example:

- Physical education: games and athletic skills practised through individual, pair and team activities, and health-related exercise;
- English: discussion, reading/writing letters, invitations, programmes and reports;
- Maths: measuring time and distance, and data handling;
- Science: links to My body topics;
- Geography: maps/plans of sports area; where were your PE shoes made?
- Art and design: posters, programmes and art theme: Sports Day;
- Personal/social education: co-operation, competition, leadership and responsibility.

How can we plan sports days to meet these cross-curricular aims and answer the concerns and doubts about the educational value of the event? Can we provide opportunities for all to succeed at their own level? Can we ensure that all participate and are kept as active as possible? Can we organise sports days within the constraints of school timetables, and sustain the interest of the children? The following models are examples of the ways sports days may be organised. Few schools will adopt such a rigid approach as the traditional model (below), preferring to adapt a more differentiated scheme (adapted model). More schools are now enjoying the challenges and rewards offered to all children in the Active PE model shown opposite.

Schools will choose events and activities best suited to their children, and which best meet the aims outlined above. Whichever model of organisation is chosen, it is a good idea to involve children in the planning process, for it will help them understand the principles involved in the event and give them an opportunity to share their ideas, needs and concerns.

The traditional model

The traditional model of sports day is a lot of people watching a few children competing in a succession of events, such as running, skipping, egg and spoon, sack, relays, etc. Sometimes children are allowed to enter a number of events, sometimes only one event. Races are often divided into boys' or girls' events, and banded according to age or year group. Some sports activities, like jumping or throwing, are often ignored. There is usually one race at a time; races are often organised in heats and then finals, with points or prizes for the winners, and perhaps a trophy for the best team or house. Parents' or toddlers' races may add interest to the occasion, but little account is taken of the special needs of individual children, and only a few children are active at any one time.

Traditional model – adapted

Many schools have adapted this traditional model to include a wider variety of events, such as ball, hoop or beanbag events, jumping and throwing events, mixed-age events, more team events and fun events such as wellie throwing, giant ball or space hopper races. It may be organised without points scored, or every child who enters scores so that all achieve some success. A wider variety of events allows for more differentiated activities and a wider range of sports experience, but this model continues the race/spectate tradition where most children remain, not active participants, but spectators.

The following models embody more successfully the principles of active PE by keeping all children active in a variety of events.

Active PE model

Example

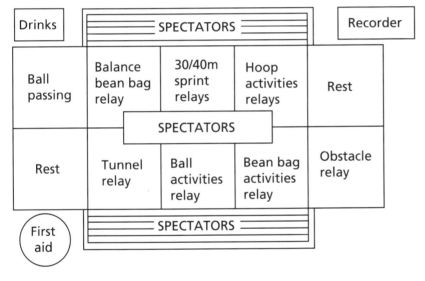

The sports area is divided into a number of stations (or events), and children rotate in groups around the circuit to each activity in turn. One teacher or adult helper is in charge of each station, with other helpers as needed. The circuit also includes opportunities for children to rest, and to have refreshments as appropriate. This approach aims to value the contribution of all children, not just the best athletes. Active sports days can be either competitive or co-operative, as in the following example. Other activities might include :

• Throwing sponge/airflow balls.
• Standing long jump.
• Any class games included on pp66–68.
• Sack, egg and spoon, skipping relays.
• Novelty races.
• Bat and ball skills.
• Childrens' invented games with set apparatus.

In schools where groups will be 30 or so in number, ensure small teams of five are active by using relays to score maximum repetitions or circuits in a set time, or first past the post, or just enjoy the activity for **fun.**

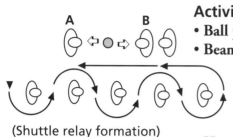

(Shuttle relay formation)

Activities

- **Ball passing**: corner spry in fives.
- **Bean bag activities**: (shuttle relay formation)
  A put down, touch B's hand who runs, picks up bag and hands to next child and so on.
- **Sprint relays**: children run as above, to touch hand of next runner.
- **Hoop activities**: as above with hoops being rolled or skipped, or with two hoops jumping from one to another over 20 m.
- **Tunnel (or weaving) relay**:

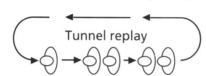

Tunnel replay

children dodge or crawl between legs to back of team and run back to place. Last child runs to front to weave or crawl to back to finish.

- **Ball activities**: in shuttle relay pattern balls can be dribbled, bounced, tossed, held before handing to next child.
- **Balance bean bag**: shuttle relay while balancing bag on head, back, shoulder or top of thigh or foot, to hand to next child.
- **Rest groups**: for use of toilet, have drinks, spectate.

You will adapt this model to suit your own situation. With active help from parents and friends it will be a fun day for all.

Checklist for sports day

The following is a checklist of aspects of organisation for a sports day. These suggestions will need to be adapted to suit your circumstances. Whole-staff planning and the involvement of children should help ensure a happy, active and successful sports day.

Half-term before
- plan the programme of events;
- plan staff/helper responsibilities;
- send out invitations/information to parents and other guests;
- check PA system (if needed);
- check markings on field (if needed);
- compile list of equipment needed;
- organise teams and entries;
- devise a wet-weather plan;
- include teaching for events in PE lessons;
- hold any extra events, eg jumping/throwing.

One week before
- send parents an information letter;
- confirm teacher/helper duties;
- display field plan for the sports day;
- agree rules for the day;
- teams chosen and practising (if possible);
- prepare recording/scoring procedures;

- plan refreshments;
- organise teams of helpers, eg for when sports are over.

On sports day
- check list of children/teams/helpers;
- prepare field for events;
- check first-aid;
- organise recording and scorecards;
- prepare refreshments;
- check field for stones, waste, etc;
- ensure children are ready changed and have been to the toilet!

After sports day
- thank helpers;
- give awards and praise;
- organise helpers to clear away apparatus;
- clear site of litter;
- review the day with staff/children involved.

Outdoor and adventurous activities

'I learn better outdoors – I think it's the fresh air'
(seven year-old on an outing)

Outdoor education involves moving, living and learning outside the classroom. Some aspects of outdoor activity may take place as part of the normal school day, at breaktimes or in timetabled sessions, and some may take the form of special visits or extra-curricular activity. A programme of study needs to be planned so that children experience a range of outdoor activities. At Key Stage 1 the National Curriculum requires that pupils should:

• explore the potential of physical activities within the immediate environment;
• undertake simple orientation activities;
• apply physical skills out of doors on suitable equipment;
• develop an awareness of basic safety practices.
(Key Stage 1 Programmes of Study, 1992)

The physical health of the child is the foundation of the child's total development. Health-related exercise should be part of every child's experience, to help maintain health, to develop their physical skills and foster all-round development. Children should be given opportunities to develop a wide range of simple movements in a variety of outdoor and adventurous activities, with and without equipment. A single unit of work should cover this key stage and could include the activities listed below:

School environment: exploring the environment within the school grounds, eg climbing frames, outdoor play equipment, grassy area, conservation area, site buildings and boundaries. Where possible, permanent equipment (conforming to British Safety Standards) should be sited on an impact-absorbing base. Examples of permanent equipment which can be used at breaktimes and lesson time for both physical and adventurous activities include:

• climbing frame;
• stepping stones or tree trunks of various heights, about 50 cm apart, for balancing, stepping, jumping from or running in and out of;
• a plank or large tree trunk for practising balancing, walking or jumping;
• a metal bar, for hanging, swinging and somersaults, about one metre from the ground;
• parallel bars on which children can climb, sit or hang;

- wooden or PVC blocks built into interesting shapes that children can climb or jump from;
- a slide, built into a mound, with proper steps, for sliding;
- an old boat that children can climb into for imaginative play;
- bushes, trees and brick flowerbeds for children to hide behind and run round;
- playground markings such as hopscotch grid, running track, 100-number square, or large map, jumping lines, geometric shapes, etc.

Local environments: exploring different environments in the locality, or a trip to a distant locality, for experience of outdoor and adventurous activity. Examples of local environments that may be suitable include:

- local park for outdoor play, with opportunities to walk, skip and run on different surfaces;
- local playground with permanent play equipment, explaining the safe use of equipment, and encouraging children to practise what they have learnt in school;
- hills provide opportunities for strenuous walking, as well as rolling down, running and games;
- water environments, eg lakes, canals, rivers, seaside, provide opportunities to link outdoor activity with other areas of study;
- conservation areas and nature trails;
- farm visits;
- town or city walks, eg a sketching trip or visit to places of interest.

Outdoor education can link with all areas of the curriculum (see p17), but has particular links with geography; the following elements relate to field work outdoors:

- observe and describe surroundings;
- follow directions, including forwards/backwards, up/down, left/right, north/south/east/west;
- follow a route on a simple map, eg of the local area, produced by teacher or child;
- visit, identify and name familiar features in the local area;
- investigate the use of land and buildings;
- identify and describe geographical features of the local environment.

Planning for outdoor activity

In planning for outdoor and adventurous activities, consideration should be given to each element of the 'plan-do-review' process:

- **Planning**: usually begins in class beforehand and questions might include: Where can we go? Why might we go there? What can we do there? How can we get there? What do we need to remember? What will we need? Who could help us? What should we look for? What should we take with us? Who should we tell about where we are going? Encourage them to share ideas with you and each other about what you/they might do, and how you/they might go about it. Ask the children to draw or chart their plans and ideas.

• **Performing**: in undertaking an outdoor or adventurous activity we should try to make it

A ctive	promoting healthy life-styles and attitudes.
C o-operative	working with and taking care of others.
T houghtful	encouraging a thoughtful approach to physical activity.
I nventive	fostering a creative response to physical challenge.
V aried	developing a variety of skills.
E njoyable	enjoying their activities in PE.

• **Reviewing**: describing what they and others are doing or have done, and how they did it. Review and discussion time can take place after an activity, or 'in recollection' after the trip or lesson is over. Questions that might be relevant include: What did you/he/she/we do? How did you/she/he/we do it? What do you think about what you/we/she/he did? According to the PoS we should encourage children to use terms that are:

  • simple: using their own words;
  • functional: describing what they see and do;
  • aesthetic: judging how well they and others have done.

Examples of outdoor activities

The following are case-studies of ways outdoor activities may be planned:

School environment: the climbing frame
A good warm-up activity for exploring the outdoor school environment is 'follow-my-leader', for example, jogging along the lines marked out on a school playground, around an obstacle course of rounders bases or behind the teacher, 'conga' style. These activities may be done in pairs, in groups or as a whole class.

Aims
• To explore the potential for physical activities using the school's outdoor climbing frame.
• To apply physical skills on the climbing frame, including upper and lower body development, balance, control, co-ordination, visual perception, body awareness, laterality and tactile perception.
• To develop an awareness of basic safety procedures on the climbing frame.

Activity

An infant class was invited to explore physical activity, in groups, on the climbing frame. Each group in turn was allowed to experiment and practise physical skills on the frame while the others made drawings of the frame and the activities they were watching.

Method

Plan, perform and review:

- Different methods of access on to the frame, using hands and feet: how many ways?
- Activities on the climbing frame can be based on the following themes: up/down, under/through, over, balancing, hanging, making shapes, linking movements and creating pathways.
- Methods of descent, eg climbing down, crawling down, sliding, jumping, hanging and dropping.

A climbing frame can be a resource for outdoor activity and adventure. It can be both a motivator and a practice station for developing and exploring many kinds of physical skill. With teacher guidance, children will learn to investigate a wider range of physical activity and develop finer motor control skills than if left solely on their own. A frame can also be a resource for exciting dramatic, creative and imaginative play. It can, for example, become a castle, an island, a ship or a space rocket. Key aspects of introducing children to the full potential of the frame will be the need for safety, physical awareness and thought for others.

Other pieces of playground apparatus may also have potential for helping children develop physical skills and movement awareness in an outdoor setting.

The local environment: a nature trail or local park

Aims
• To explore the environment from a variety of perspectives – physical, geographical, biological and aesthetic.
• To undertake simple orientation activities.
• Appreciation of the environment, and of the value of health-related exercise.

Activity
A nature trail through a local enviroment was planned by the class teacher, where children were encouraged to use all their senses in discovering more about the natural world and themselves.

Method
Each group of children was led by an adult (teacher or parent) along the trail. Various stops were selected for children to use their senses in the investigation of the environment, including:

• Being blindfolded and walking part of thc trail led by an adult holding a rope.
• Touching the trees, feeling the barks, and the textures of walls.
• Listening to sounds in an open area.
• Walking on different surfaces and listening to the sound of their feet.
• Smelling flowering shrubs, and herbs.
• Looking at and identifying key features seen near and far.

At the end of the trail children were asked to find their way back to the beginning from the clues and features picked up during the walk. As a follow-up activity children drew the trail on a plan of the site, showing the features they remembered and adding their own observations. On a large map they described their outing to the rest of the school.

A distant environment: a beach trip

A trip involving two classes of infants, aged from five to seven, was planned to take advantage of a special excursion offer from British Rail.

Aims

• To explore, through physical and other activity, a beach environment.
• To experience physical activity in the water.
• To develop an awareness of the need for safety practices.

Activity

Pre-visit preparation included study of shells, rock pools and the sea, and training in water safety.

A large number of helpers were recruited to allow one adult to every three or four children. Equipment included study materials such as books, collecting jars, plastic bags, swimming gear and games equipment (plus a complete change of clothes!). During the journey children counted bridges, tunnels, stations and how many different kinds of animal they could see. At the beach they changed into swimwear before embarking on beach activities.

Method

The programme of beach activities included:

• A treasure or scavenger hunt in and around the rock pools to collect interesting specimens, including pebbles, seaweed, shells, etc.
• A pre-lunch paddle or swim in the sea (tide tables having been consulted beforehand); some adults in the water, some watching from the waterside with whistle to signal recall.
• Lunch (after changing), rest and complete clearing of rubbish.
• A sand-and-pebble/seaweed/shell castle-making competition.
• Beach games with small apparatus, and some races.

Follow-up work in school included marking out the journey on the school playground, showing the railway track and stations, and children journeying along the rails to the stations of their choice.

For Assessment of outdoor and adventurous activities see pp103, 107. For Resources for outdoor education see pp117, 124.

Swimming

' I wish I was a fish – swimming would be so much easier!'
(six year-old)

Swimming is not a compulsory subject in the National Curriculum at Key Stage 1, but some schools will include swimming activities as part of their curriculum for infant children. A few children may enter school already able to swim. For the great majority of children, early water play experiences will be useful as confidence-boosting activities from the reception year onwards.

The aim of the National Curriculum is that at the end of Key Stage 2 'all pupils should be able to swim unaided at least 25 metres and demonstrate an understanding of water safety'. Swimming is a vital, potentially life-saving, activity. Therefore it is important that swimming begins as early as possible. The Progamme of Study for Key Stage 2 states that children should:

- learn and know the codes of hygiene and courtesy for using swimming pools;
- be given opportunities to develop confidence in water, be taught how to rest in water, how to float and to adopt support positions;
- be taught a variety of means of propulsion using either arms or legs or both, and develop effective and efficient swimming strokes on front and back;
- be taught water safety and the principles of water safety to assess the nature, visibility and location of water hazards in a variety of conditions;
- learn universal skills appropriate to their competence in water and evaluate their own abilities and limitations;
- be encouraged to assess their swimming and waterskills efficiency against a range of activities;
- explore the elements of movement in the water through simple games;
- be made aware of the role of swimming and water safety skills in supporting other water-based activities and activities near water.
(PE in the National Curriculum, 1992)

A programme of swimming for infant children could include the following units of work:

- water play to build confidence;
- rules of water safety and hygiene;
- getting in and out of the pool;
- moving in and under the water;
- moving through the water, supporting the body with and without aids;
- water games to play for confidence and fun;
- activities and stroke development leading to swimming.

Resources needed for swimming with infants include access to a learner pool, or a paddling pool with warm, clear water to a depth of approximately 30 cm. Buoyancy aids for use in the pool should include a variety of balls, rings and shapes that float, as well as inflatable armbands and rings which are of a suitable size and a comfortable fit for your children. There should be sufficient floatboards for each child to use, if needed. It is best to teach children in blocks of 6–12 sessions so that continuity and progression are maintained.

The most valuable resources for swimming are, of course, the adult helpers – teachers and qualified swimming instructors. When the children first start, it is important for them to have a swimming teacher who knows their needs. If you are not a qualified swimming teacher add another string to your bow and do your children a favour by gaining the qualification at an ASA teacher course, often held at local pools. It should be remembered that very timid or disabled children may need an additional adult in the water. Even if you are not qualified, pool staff will often welcome your assistance by the poolside.

Plan early to arrange visits to a local authority swimming pool, and try to go either at the beginning or end of a school session to save curriculum time. You could arrange for parents to collect children, thus saving on transport costs.

What to teach

A typical lesson might consist of:
- Before entry: reminders about safety, hygiene, conduct and lesson content.
- Water entry and introductory fun activity.
- Water activities including moving, floating and breathing.
- Water games.

Children will need a warm and well-ordered changing area (parent helpers are often very useful here). Try to arrange sole use of the learner/shallow end pool if possible during the lesson; check that armbands, floats, etc are readily available and accessible at key points around the pool, and that the water is 28–30°C. Water should not be deeper than chest height (about 90 cm) for beginners, and the steps should be at the shallow end. Children should never be allowed in or near the pool unattended. A qualified life-saver should always be with them.

Fig 10: Indoor water play

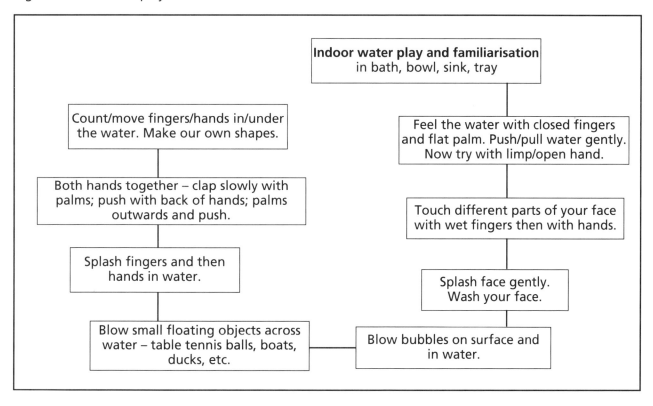

Fig 11: Outdoor water play

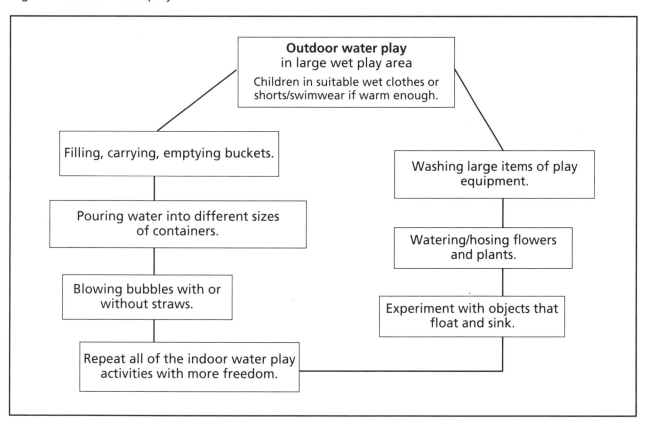

Fig 12: Paddling pool activities

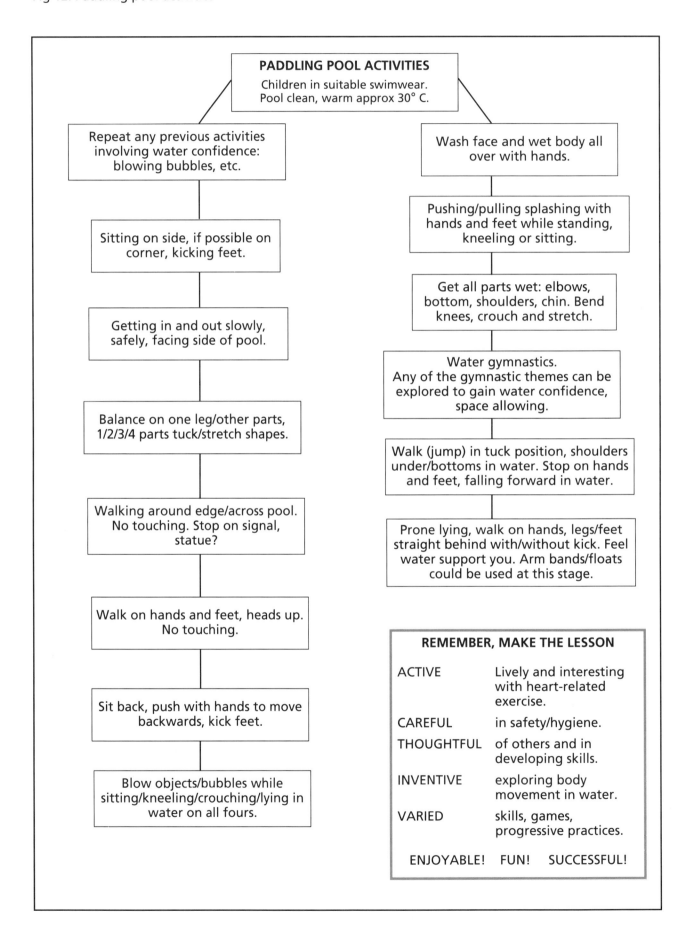

PADDLING POOL ACTIVITIES
Children in suitable swimwear.
Pool clean, warm approx 30° C.

Repeat any previous activities
involving water confidence:
blowing bubbles, etc.

Sitting on side, if possible on
corner, kicking feet.

Getting in and out slowly,
safely, facing side of pool.

Balance on one leg/other parts,
1/2/3/4 parts tuck/stretch shapes.

Walking around edge/across pool.
No touching. Stop on signal,
statue?

Walk on hands and feet, heads up.
No touching.

Sit back, push with hands to move
backwards, kick feet.

Blow objects/bubbles while
sitting/kneeling/crouching/lying in
water on all fours.

Wash face and wet body all
over with hands.

Pushing/pulling splashing with
hands and feet while standing,
kneeling or sitting.

Get all parts wet: elbows,
bottom, shoulders, chin. Bend
knees, crouch and stretch.

Water gymnastics.
Any of the gymnastic themes can be
explored to gain water confidence,
space allowing.

Walk (jump) in tuck position, shoulders
under/bottoms in water. Stop on hands
and feet, falling forward in water.

Prone lying, walk on hands, legs/feet
straight behind with/without kick. Feel
water support you. Arm bands/floats
could be used at this stage.

REMEMBER, MAKE THE LESSON

ACTIVE	Lively and interesting with heart-related exercise.
CAREFUL	in safety/hygiene.
THOUGHTFUL	of others and in developing skills.
INVENTIVE	exploring body movement in water.
VARIED	skills, games, progressive practices.

ENJOYABLE!   FUN!   SUCCESSFUL!

Learner pool: water entry and introductory activities

Don't rush children into the water. Timid ones may need time to watch, to sit and dangle feet in the water, and to kick or splash the water before joining in. Keep instructions to children brief and simple and use lots of praise and encouragement during activities. Repeat any paddling pool activities that are appropriate, and try to make their experience of water fun. Here are some water entry and introductory activities:

- Children walk down steps into shallow pool, holding the rail (if there is one), or slide feet first, on tummy into the water.
- Stand in water and 'wash' face with it.
- Put shoulders under water.
- Bob up and down in the water, holding rail with two hands, one hand and then no hands!
- Walk round edge of pool, holding rail with one or both hands. Change direction on signal.
- Splash water over the body – is it best to do it with your fingers open or closed?
- Face the rail, hold with both hands, bob up and down, put shoulders under, then chin, and hair.

As confidence grows, these activities can be repeated away from the rail in a clear water space. After the water entry and introductory activities it may be appropriate to play one of the following games or skill activities.

Water games for gaining confidence

The following are some water games to help children gain in water confidence. They are especially useful as beginning or ending activities.

Boats

A team of five or six children stand in line. Each child holds the shoulders or waist of the child in front. When ready, the leader walks into spaces in the water, leading the 'boat' of children linked together in line. Change leaders on signal. Can the 'boat' move backwards?

Simon says

Children repeat the teacher's actions at poolside. All start with five points; no one drops out if they do not repeat the right action, but lose a point through a false move.

Lifeboats

Teacher names the sides of the pool as parts of a boat or points to the direction of travel. Children walk/run/hop/jump to the side indicated by the teacher. If 'lifeboat!' is called children jump up/duck under water/ jump on the spot (or perform another given task).

Saved

The pool is scattered with various floats or swimming aids. Children move freely about the pool; on a signal children grab the nearest float to help them move to the nearest aid, or they must find a float of special shape or colour to 'save' themselves and reach safety.

Splash! Splosh!

Children stand in two lines, back to back, one to two metres apart. One line is the Splashes, the other line is the Sploshes. On teacher's shout of 'SPLASH!' or 'SPLOSH!' the line called moves quickly to the side rail before the other line can turn and catch them.

Beachcomber

Teacher scatters the pool with floats or swimming aids. Working together, children must collect as many floats/aids from the surface, one at a time, to place on the poolside at the teacher's feet (eg in a basket). Teacher keeps count and can toss floats back into the water when a given time (say 30 seconds) is up.

Pearldiver

This game is similar to Beachcomber, but the children have to retrieve sinking objects (coins, spoons) from the bottom of the pool

Tag games

- **Touch**: child wearing armbands moves across the pool to touch as many others as possible. On signal, the last one touched becomes the next chaser.
- **Release**: chaser wearing armband chases and freezes tagged children, who can only be released by a touch from a releaser wearing two armbands (when more confident, release can be by touching a foot or moving through legs).
- **Chain**: chaser joins hands with tagged players. When four are joined, children divide into pairs and so on.

Basking whales

Two or three children blow bubbles in the centre of the pool (whales). Other children try to cross to the other side. On signal, 'whales' tag the crossing children who can escape by reaching/touching the opposite rail or a floating object thrown in the water.

Crafty captain

Children (the crew) line up at opposite end of pool to the teacher (the 'crafty captain in his/her cabin'), back facing the class. Children walk, shoulders under the water, until the captain suddenly turns round to try and catch (see) anyone moving, or with their shoulders out of the water. 'Caught' crew take two or three paces back before restarting, and trying to reach the captain's cabin. Child who reaches the captain's cabin wins.

Relay games

These can be enjoyable, if winning is not too important. Try counting the number of widths in a set time rather than having positions. Teams of four are best, with two pairs facing each other on opposite sides of the pool, to reduce waiting time. Relay games to play include:

• Walking, or walking with shoulders under water.
• Nosing or chesting a floating ball.
• Holding a float and kicking legs.
• Swimming doggy paddle.
• Walk or doggy paddle through a hoop held vertically in the water.

Chanting games

Rhymes such as 'Ring o' roses' and 'Pop goes the weasel' are excellent played in a circle. Children, hands joined, walk round singing/chanting. On the punch lines 'All fall down!' or 'Pop goes the weasel!' the children can submerge, jump up high, sit on bottom, etc depending on confidence or ability. Invent other games, singing songs you know, moving through and ducking under the water. Singing can help calm nervous children – and teachers!

Learning to swim

After water confidence has been gained through a variety of confidence-building activities, learning to swim can begin in easy stages, slowly improving with practice, as follows:

Breathing: introductory activities

One of the problems to overcome in learning to swim is breathing in water. Build up confidence in breathing in and under water by:

• Blowing objects through the water to a partner, eg table tennis balls.
• Cup hands full of water, put your lips to the water and blow hard.
• Hold rail, bend knees, take a deep breath, eyes closed, put your head under and blow bubbles.
• Try the above with your hands on the bottom of the shallow pool.
• With head under, as above, can you hum or make noises under water?
• Try putting your head under the water, with eyes open, and count the fingers shown by a partner.
• Free-standing in the water, deep breath, head under, blow bubbles, come up for air and repeat several times.
• Make different shapes in the water, eg curl/stretch/twist. What shapes can you make? Which help you float in water?

Propulsion through water

Swimming depends on propelling the body through the water. A shallow learner pool is an ideal place to practice:

• Holding the rail, children make waves with their chest/shoulders,

- Release hold of the rail; make waves sweeping arms, palms outstretched, forwards and backwards.
- Practise being wading ducks, or leaping frogs, keeping shoulders under water, standing on one leg.
- Practise being boats, gulls, snakes, submarines, etc with suitable actions, encouraging shoulders under water, getting faces wet, bending knees, taking feet off the bottom and moving forwards.

Shallow water propulsion

Shallow water, as in paddling pools, is useful for encouraging children to lie full length and propel their bodies through the water. The following are some activities for propulsion through shallow water:

- Touch the bottom of the pool with one/two hands.
- Walk on your hands and both feet/one foot through the water, keeping your chin above the surface.
- In suitable depth place both hands on the bottom and trail one/both legs behind.
- Practise the above action with kicking legs.

At this stage consider armbands to free arms for dog paddle movements.

- Sit down on pool bottom, chin above water. Hold arms rigid, lift bottom up with legs out in front; keep tummy up to float in water.

- Practise the above, walking backwards on hands, and kicking feet.
- Lie back with a float under each arm and practise the above.

Propulsion using floats and armbands

Progression can be made by use of armbands to give children confidence in trying a variety of activities in the water. As skills and confidence develop, practise the activities without a buoyancy support.

- Holding a float under each arm, hop on one leg then the other, to leap clear of the pool bottom.
- Practise the above kicking out like a frog, and making cycling movements.
- Hold floats and make different shapes with your body in the water on front and back; keep both feet up off the bottom of the pool.
- Hold float with two hands in front; lean forward to hop on one foot.
- Practise the above, gliding through water to the rail, and from the rail with one leg-push to a partner.
- Hold floats under arms, lie back in water; push off from rail keeping tummy up and glide to a waiting partner.

For further ideas and activities on teaching swimming, including the development of different swimming strokes, diving, water safety activities, refer to *Active PE* Book 2.

Assessing and recording achievement

'Assessment of pupils' attainment is a continous process and is integral to all teaching and learning. It will inform teachers and pupils (and parents) about progress, and help to identify learner strengths, weaknesses and needs.'

(Non-Statutory Guidance in PE, 1992)

Your day-to-day observations in the PE lesson will tell you much about your children's physical achievements and capabilities. Some of these assessments will need to be recorded, as 'teachers will need to refer to their own continuous assessment during the key stage to report on a pupil's achievement at the end of the key stage' *(Non-Statutory Guidance in PE 1992)*. The principles that should govern record-keeping in PE can be summed up as:

Fig 13: Assessment in PE

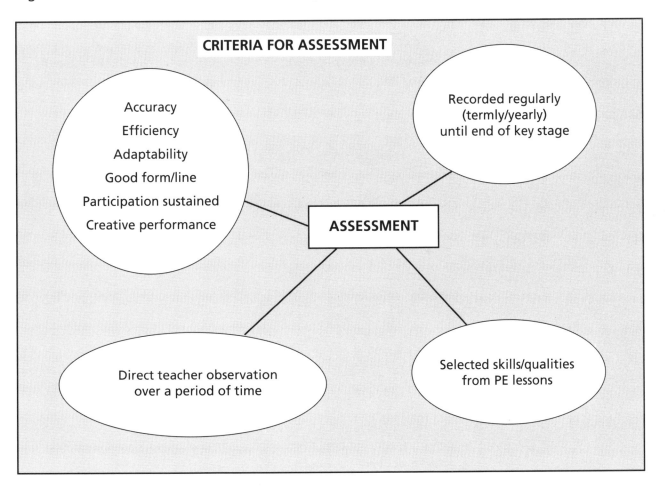

CRITERIA FOR ASSESSMENT

Accuracy
Efficiency
Adaptability
Good form/line
Participation sustained
Creative performance

Recorded regularly
(termly/yearly)
until end of key stage

ASSESSMENT

Direct teacher observation
over a period of time

Selected skills/qualities
from PE lessons

The following record sheets are designed to make your task easier by offering ways of recording only the key elements of progress that occur within the normal PE programme. Progress can be recorded termly, yearly or at the end of the key stage. They are photocopiable, and you may wish to add to or amend them to suit your own needs. Use whatever recording method suits you. The two following methods are simple and allow for recording of progression:

a) / = experienced activity   ✓ = achieved activity

or

b) / = below average   L = average ability

△ = above average   △ = excellent

The record sheets include space for comment on such areas as growth, attitude, maturity and special needs. They also include teacher assessment records for individual children in the key areas of PE, and class records of achievements and experiences in PE. These records include opportunities to make a qualitative assessment, and to make particular comments on successes or difficulties encountered. There are also sample record sheets for self-assessment in PE for the children in your class. These are photocopiable, and may be adapted or developed to suit your needs.

For practical purposes assessment and record keeping should be kept to a minimum. The record sheets can be completed at the end of the term/ year/key stage.

(Note: The self assessment sheets are adapted from *Recording Achievement in Primary Schools* by R Fisher. Published by Simon & Schuster, 1991.)

Teacher assessment records

Class records

Gymnastics
Suggested skills and qualities:

- Flexibility: bending, stretching and extension of the body.
- Agility: spring, speed and lightness.
- Body control: balance, landing, posture and poise.
- Creativity: exploration and inventiveness.

Dance
Suggested skills and qualities:

- Body actions: dance movements using different parts of the body.
- Form: body line, control and poise.
- Expressive quality: sensitivity to mood and stimuli.
- Creativity: exploration and inventiveness.

Games and athletics
Suggested skills and qualities:

- Running: action, speed and dodging.
- Jumping: spring, lift and landing.
- Throwing (small ball): under/overarm.
- Ball skills (large ball): catching, passing and dribbling.
- Striking (bat shapes): co-ordination and accuracy.
- Inventiveness: exploring/creating new ideas for games activity.

Outdoor activities
Suggested skills and qualities:

- Planning: discussing ideas/plans, understanding about safety.
- Practising: sustaining activity, working with others, improving performance.
- Reviewing: recognising/describing/evaluating effects of activity.

Swimming
Suggested skills and qualities:

- Water confidence: water entry, playing games in water.
- Moving underwater: face/head under, touch bottom with hands.
- Moving on front (with aids): swim on front with armbands, float, etc.
- Moving on back (with aids): swim on back with armbands, floats, etc.
- Swimming: eg 10–25 m, on front/back, unaided.

RECORD OF ACHIEVEMENT – GYMNASTICS

CLASS/YEAR...

	Names	Flexibility	Agility	Body control	Creativity	Comments
1						
2						
3						
4						
5						
6						
7						
8						
9						
10						
11						
12						
13						
14						
15						
16						
17						
18						
19						
20						
21						
22						
23						
24						
25						
26						
27						
28						
29						
30						

RECORD OF ACHIEVEMENT – DANCE

CLASS/YEAR...

	Names	Body actions	Form	Expressive quality	Creative movement	Comments
1						
2						
3						
4						
5						
6						
7						
8						
9						
10						
11						
12						
13						
14						
15						
16						
17						
18						
19						
20						
21						
22						
23						
24						
25						
26						
27						
28						
29						
30						

RECORD OF ACHIEVEMENT – Games and Athletics

CLASS/YEAR...

	Names	Running	Jumping	Throwing (small ball)	Ball skills (large ball)	Striking	Inventiveness	Comments
1								
2								
3								
4								
5								
6								
7								
8								
9								
10								
11								
12								
13								
14								
15								
16								
17								
18								
19								
20								
21								
22								
23								
24								
25								
26								
27								
28								
29								
30								

RECORD OF ACHIEVEMENT – Outdoor and adventurous activities

CLASS/YEAR...

	Names	Activities/comments
1		
2		
3		
4		
5		
6		
7		
8		
9		
10		
11		
12		
13		
14		
15		
16		
17		
18		
19		
20		
21		
22		
23		
24		
25		
26		
27		
28		
29		
30		

RECORD OF ACHIEVEMENT – Swimming

CLASS/YEAR..

	Names	Water confidence	Move under water	Front (with aids)	Back (with aids)	10/25m (front)	10/25m (back)	Comments
1								
2								
3								
4								
5								
6								
7								
8								
9								
10								
11								
12								
13								
14								
15								
16								
17								
18								
19								
20								
21								
22								
23								
24								
25								
26								
27								
28								
29								
30								

RECORD OF ACHIEVEMENT – Physical education

NAME...DATE..........................

End of key stage statements for Key Stage 1:

Pupils should be able to:

a) plan and perform safely a range of simple actions and linked movements in response to given tasks and stimuli;

b) practise and improve their performance;

c) describe what they and others are doing;

d) recognise the effects of physical activities on their bodies.

Examples of progress/achievement

General comments

Signed..**Class teacher**

Individual child records

Annual record of achievement in PE

Self-assessment records (by the child)

Children who have difficulties in writing can draw and/or have their words scribed by a teacher or helper.

What I can do in PE (p111)

This record sheet invites the child to record areas of success in PE, eg new skills, games played, times and distances achieved, etc.

What I did in PE (p112)

This record sheet invites the child to reflect on a PE experience, or series of experiences, and to record, describe and evaluate the experience(s).

My record of achievement in PE (p113)

This record sheet invites the child to write a report based on a series of questions about PE, for their own annual, half-yearly or termly report on PE. (An alternative approach would be to ask children to suggest questions/categories for such a report.)

My report of the year (p114)

This record sheet offers children the opportunity to write and/or draw what they have done, enjoyed and achieved in their year of PE lessons. (Discuss or display the different elements of the PE programme they may wish to comment on: gymnastics, dance, games, athletics, outdoor activities and swimming.)

WHAT I CAN DO IN PE

Name..Date of birth..............

Achievement	Date

WHAT I DID IN PE

Name...Date..............

What I did

What was good about it?

My record of achievement in PE

Name..School year..................

My school...............................My teacher..................

What I can do in PE

The best things about me in PE

What I like in PE

What games I play

How I have improved this year

What I want to do next year

Signed...Date..............................

My report of the year in PE

Name...Year..............

Special needs

Teachers need to be very aware of all kinds of physical disability that may present themselves in the mainstream school, from the very timid or poorly co-ordinated child, to the child with a specific physical disability.

Most children with a physical disability need more exercise than National Curriculum requirements. They should take part in all activities alongside other children where possible, so that they adapt naturally and use their bodies in the most effective way. It may be that a Statement of Special Educational Needs will have been made before the child enters primary school, and additional classroom support may be available. However, there will be some children with such a statement who do not have special needs in PE, and many children with special needs in PE who are seen to be making satisfactory progress in all other areas of the curriculum. There are also some children who are especially gifted at PE, or at aspects of PE, who will, at some time in their school career, need special coaching in out-of-school clubs if their talents are to be fully realised.

The experimental and challenge approaches that are part of good practice in PE are particularly suited to children with different needs and abilities, although some special provision for children with special needs may have to be made. The suggestions below may prove helpful.

Physically disabled
• Let children practise the skills already learned/the abilities they have.
• Look for planning/leadership/evaluative skills– not just performance.
• Encourage mobility exercises advised by physiotherapist.
• Adapt apparatus and explore new ideas to suit needs (other children can be encouraged to plan this).
• Considerations: size and weight of balls; size, weight and width of bats; height of benches, tables, targets; distance of target, partner; wheelchair activities/non-wheelchair activities.

Hearing-impaired children
• Face the children, reduce background noise and speak slowly and clearly.
• Agree a touch signal that all can use for 'stop' or 'watch'.
• Demonstrate activity when appropriate.
• Move with child/hold hand where necessary.
• Encourage use of vibration/rhythm experiences in movement.

Visually impaired children
- Agree a stop signal for all to use; use a child's name before speaking.
- If possible provide brightly coloured/shiny/crinkly apparatus that can be picked out, **felt** and **heard** when used.
- Use small equipment with bright colours and different textures.
- Encourage children to listen and feel their way to apparatus.
- Use partner Buddy system where appropriate.
- Encourage running in free, open spaces at first.

Moderate learning difficulties/poor motor co-ordination
- Clear, simple instructions; lots of praise and motivation.
- Set clear achievement targets; expect them to be achieved in easy stages.
- Active adult support in gross and locomotor activities. Severe cases should be referred for statement/physiotherapist help.
- Use adapted equipment where necessary.

Asthma sufferers are encouraged to take medication and exercise in order to combat an attack. Advice from parents and doctor is essential.

Diabetes sufferers can take part in all activities, but staff must be aware of child's eating pattern/insulin reaction. Watch for signs of breathlessness, dizziness or discomfort.

Epileptics are encouraged to take part in PE activities, but there may be risk situations to avoid, or in which a partner should be employed.

Resources for PE

The following are some suggested resources for PE with infants:

Indoor area – the school hall

In most schools, the hall will be a multi-purpose area for lunch, assembly, music and drama as well as for PE activities. Ensure that it is safe for physical activity. Check for any wet or slippery patches, especially after lunch, and that any furniture does not project dangerously into the teaching area. If physical activity is to take place in the playground, it too, must be checked for hidden dangers before the session begins.

Large apparatus for PE is best spaced round the sides of the hall for ease of access; labels on the walls will help to remind everyone of its position. Small apparatus and games equipment can be stored in a wide cupboard. It may also be possible to have a secure shed or outbuilding near the playground or field for games equipment.

Outdoor areas

An outdoor play area could include:
• a grassed area, partly banked if possible, and with a gardening/growing area;
• areas for sand and water play (sandpit with lockable cover if possible);
• a climbing frame, ideally with some flexibility to alter angles and positions, eg with steps, planks, net, tyres, 'window' frames, flat areas, ladder, and safe landing area;
• tree stumps, stepping stones, large tunnels, etc to encourage climbing, stepping, crawling, jumping, balance, walking, and co-ordination skills.

The playground
Check regularly that the play surface is safe and free from potential dangers such as loose gravel, glass or animal waste (for further information see *Playground Safety Guidelines* available from DE, Sanctuary Buildings, Great Smith St, London SW1 3BT).

Playgrounds can be made stimulating areas for both imaginative and recreational play. For ideas for activities on playframes and climbing apparatus see Outdoor and adventurous activities (p90).

Markings
The following markings on the play area (fig 24) can be used during PE sessions, when appropriate, and can encourage children to practice lesson activities during playtimes. It is not intended that all these markings be included on one playground. Turn the design of playground markings into a learning opportunity by discussing possible designs with children. Ask older children to draw their own markings for playground games. Try to involve children in the decisions you or colleagues make about playground markings and play apparatus.

Fig 24 Some playground markings for PE

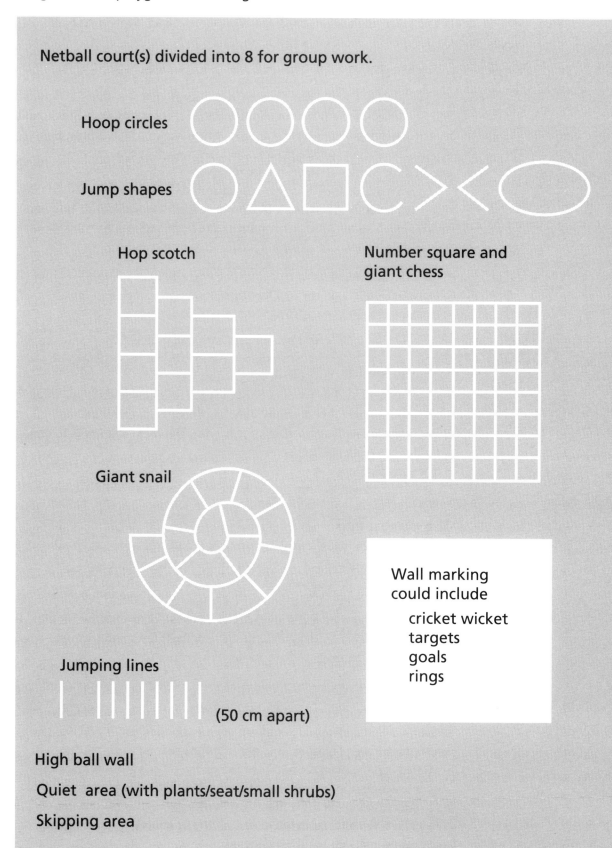

Netball court(s) divided into 8 for group work.

Hoop circles

Jump shapes

Hop scotch

Number square and giant chess

Giant snail

Wall marking could include
  cricket wicket
  targets
  goals
  rings

Jumping lines

(50 cm apart)

High ball wall

Quiet area (with plants/seat/small shrubs)

Skipping area

Gymnastics

Apparatus

Gymnastic apparatus should, where possible, be light, adjustable, and of good quality. When stored, it should be easily accessible, and checked regularly for safety. The following is a list of basic gymnastic apparatus:

- foldaway climbing frame, bars and ropes;
- round or hexagonal agility table;
- stacking, rectangular agility tables;
- ladder, two trestle trees, low balance beam, wooden or padded planks;
- three padded stools;
- four balance benches;
- twelve agility mats (in four colours);
- safety landing mat (for JM/I schools);
- mat trolleys can be useful for transporting mats, but can be troublesome if quick access/storage is required. Other possibilities include small mats (approximately 100x60 cm), hexagonal mats, or an adjustable bar box.

Further reading

BAALPE (1990), *Safe Practice in PE*
Buckland, D (1970), *Gymnastics* (Heinemann)
Carroll, H and Manners, H (1992), *Gymnastics 7–11* (Falmer Press)
Jackman, J and Currier, B (1992), *Gymnastic Skills and Games* (Black)
Williams, A (1987), *Curriculum Gymnastics* (Hodder & Stoughton)
Wetton, P (1992), *Practical Guides: Physical Education* (Scholastic)

Useful addresses

- PE Association, Ling House, Unit 5, Western Court, Bromley Street, Birmingham B94 4AN
- Health Education Council, Hamilton House, Mabledon Place, London WC1H 9TX
- British Heart Foundation Jump Rope Scheme, Dept of PE & Sports Studies, Loughborough University, Loughborough, Leicestershire LE11 3TU

Dance

Equipment

Dance equipment could include:
- a robust, good quality record/cassette player or midi system;
- a small cassette player for flexible class use;
- a variety of tuned and untuned percussion instruments, eg tambourine, drum, triangle, chime bars, castanets, coconut shells, cymbals, maracas, shakers and children's class-made instruments

Music

• a range of tapes, CDs or discs for dance, including examples from pop, rock, soul, jazz, TV themes, BBC sound effects, and collections of music from many cultures. Suggestions for classical music suitable for dance include:

Arnold: *English and Scottish Dances*
Bach: *Air on a G string*
Bernstein: *West Side Story*
Bizet: *Jeux D'Enfants*
Borodin: *Polovtsian Dances*
Chopin: *Minute Waltz*
Copland: *Appalachian Spring (canon on Lord of the Dance), Rodeo/Billy the Kid*
Debussy: *The Children's Corner Suite*
Dukas: *The Sorcerer's Apprentice*
da Falla: *Ritual Fire Dance (from El Amo Brujo)*
Glass: *Powaqqatsi*
Grieg: *Peer Gynt Suite (In the Hall of the Mountain King)*
Handel: *Arrival of the Queen of Sheba*
Herold: *La Fille mal Gardée (Clog Dance)*
Holst: *The Planets Suite*
Ibert: *Circus/Invitation to Dance*
Jean Michel Jarre: *selections*
Scott Joplin: *The Sting, Elite Syncopations*
Rimsky Korsakov: *Cappriccio Espagnol, Flight of the Bumble Bee*
John Lanchbery: *Tales of Beatrix Potter*
Mozart: *March no 1 in D*
Mussorgsky: *Night on a Bare Mountain, Pictures at an Exhibition*
Prokofiev: *Peter & the Wolf, Romeo & Juliet*
Ravel: *Bolero*
Saint-Saens: *Carnival of the Animals*
Sousa: marches, eg *Stars and Stripes Forever*
Tchaikovsky: *Nutcracker Suite*
Strauss: *Radetsky March*
Vivaldi: *Four Seasons*
Warlock: *Capriol Suite*
Vaughan Williams: *Fantasia on Greensleeves*

Poetry sources for dance

Poetry books with suitable poems as a stimulus for dance include:

Baldwin and Whitehead, 1972, *That way and this:Poetry for Creative Dance* (Chatto & Windus)

Fisher, R (ed) anthologies: *Amazing Monsters, Funny Folk, Ghosts Galore, Witch Words, Pet Poems, Minibeasts* (Faber and Faber)

Rosen, M (ed), 1991, *The Kingfisher Book of Children's Poetry* (Kingfisher Books)

Slater, 1990, *A Ring o' Roses: Poems for Movement and Dance* (Northcote House)

Further reading on dance

Arts Council: *Dance in Schools* (Arts Council Guidance on Dance Education, 1993)

BBC: *Let's Dance* – a handbook for teachers by Mary Harlow and Linda Rolfe

BBC: *Look! Look what I can do!* by Kate Harrison

Violet Bruce: *Movement and Dance in the Primary School* (Open University Press, 1988)

Harrison, K, *Bright Ideas: Dance and Movement* (Scholastic)

Mary Lowden: *Dancing to Learn* (Falmer Press, 1989)

Joan Russell: *Creative Dance in the Primary School* (Northcote House, 1992)

Rosamund Shreeves: *Children Dancing* (Ward Lock, 1990)

Useful addresses for dance

English Folk Dance and Song Society, Cecil Sharp House, 2 Regents Park Road, London NW1 7AY

Primrose Education Resources, White Cross, Lancaster LA1 4DQ

Coomber Electronic Equipment, Croft Walk, Worcester WR1 3NZ

Games and athletics

Equipment

The following is a list of basic games equipment. There should be sufficient equipment for every child in the class to use an item each of:

- bean bags (in four colours);
- plastic balls, 12 cm diameter, (four colours);
- plastic balls 20 cm diameter (four colours);
- plastic rugby balls (sizes 3/4);
- small foam balls;
- tennis or rubber balls;
- small bats;
- skipping ropes (various sizes);
- hoops (60 cm and 90 cm);
- cones for markers;
- nets/bins/wire baskets for holding balls, etc;
- games equipment trolley;
- trolley for hoops;
- playground chalk;
- **FIRST-AID CASE.**

Suppliers of PE equipment
include the following:

Hestair Hope
St Phillips Drive
Royston
Oldham CL2 6AG

Evans
Mercury House
Sutherland Road
Longton ST3 1JD

NES (Davies)
17 Ludlow Hill Road
West Bridgford
Nottingham NG2 6HD

ASCO Education
ASCO House
19 Lockwood way
Parkside Lane
Leeds LD11 5TH

Soft Play
Beauer Foam Products
Bluebell Close
Alfreton
Derby DE55 4RD

Sutcliffe Leisure
Sandbeds Trading Estate
Dewsbury road
Ossett
West Yorkshire WF5 9ND

Useful starter packs for all games are available from Sutcliffe Leisure.

Outdoor and adventurous activities

It is important to review the environment for learning opportunities; this means the school environment and other local environments. It is helpful if colleagues share their ideas and resources, perhaps to create resource boxes of ideas, information and materials on 'Our school' and 'Our local area'. Resources for outdoor education could include:

- maps – created by teachers, other adults or children;
- trails – things to see and do on a local walk;
- visual information – pictures, photos and drawings about the environment;
- trip plans – how past trips and outdoor activities have been organised;
- topic plans – curricular and cross-curricular planning charts or webs;
- school policies – related to outdoor education;
- resource lists – books, artefacts, equipment, addresses and people to contact who might help.

Swimming

Resources for swimming
- learner pool which contains shallow water and deep water;
- buoyancy aids: a variety of plastic/rubber balls, rubber rings and shapes, inflatable armbands and rings, sufficient floatboards for each child and extra swimming caps for children;
- diving discs, hoops (and weighted stands), weighted toys, and light plastic balls.

Further reading on swimming
ASA and STA Handbooks
ASA's *Teaching of Swimming, and Coaching Level 1*
Geegan A and Noble, J, *Swimming Games and Activities* (Black)
Hardy, C, *Handbook for the Teacher of Swimming* (Pelham Books, 1987)
Know the game: Swimming (Black)
Know the Game: Diving (Black)

Useful addresses
- Amateur Swimming Association (Publications), Harold Fern House, Derby Square, Loughborough LE11 0AL
- Royal Life Saving Society, Mountbatten House, Studeley, Warwickshire BB0 7NN
- Swimming Teachers Association, Anchor House, Borch St, Walsall, West Midlands W52 8HZ

Index